The Power of Attitude

By Dr. Mabel Joshua-Amadi

Filament
Publishing

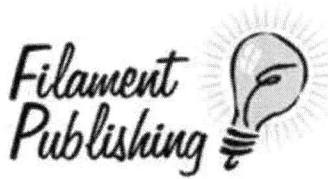

Published by Filament Publishing Ltd
16, Croydon Road, Waddon,
Croydon, Surrey, CRO 4PA UK
Telephone +44 (0)20 8688 2598
Fax +44 (0)20 7183 7186
info@filamentpublishing.com
www.filamentpublishing.com

Printed by Berforts Group - Stevenage and Hastings
Distributed by Gardners

ISBN 978-1-905493-58-6

I would like to dedicate this book
to my parents and to Edna Whitehouse

"The greatest discovery of all time is that a person can change his future by merely changing his mental attitude."
Oprah Winfrey

"Nothing can stop the man with the right mental attitude from achieving his goal; nothing on earth can help the man with the wrong mental attitude."
Thomas Jefferson

"A positive attitude can really make dreams come true - it did for me."
David Bailey

"The winner's edge is not in gifted birth, high IQ, or in talent. The winner's edge is all in attitude, not aptitude. Attitude is the criterion for success."
Denis Waitley

Acknowledgements

First I would like to thank my Teacher for His inspiration, guidance, encouragement, motivation and assistance throughout the writing of this book.

I must also thank my parents, Huldah and Joshua U. Amadi who believed in me and sustained me over the years with their love and prayers.

Thank you to my teacher, Edna Whitehouse, who taught me the benefits of patient persistence and helped to get me on the first rung of personal achievement

I would also like to thank my family for their patience, understanding and support through the years of seclusion, studies and writing.

I would like to thank my publisher, Mr. Christopher Day, whose invaluable insights delayed the publication of an earlier manuscript and helped to enrich this book.

Thanks also goes to Zara Thatcher for her editorial help that simply turned the whole manuscript into magic.

I would like to thank all those who gave their time and contributed to refining the attitude questionnaire and survey.

I would like to thank all those in my life whose attitude provided the inspiration for this book. I thank you very much for without you none of this would have been possible.

Finally, I thank you, the reader, for your courage in seeking to review your attitude and maybe use it to heal from the past unto wholeness and happiness.

Dr. Mabel Joshua-Amadi

Dr. Mabel Joshua-Amadi is a qualified medical doctor, who undertook post-graduate studies at the School of Hygiene and Tropical Medicine, London, gaining MB BS; DTMH. She served as a physician for twenty years, ten of them as a medical director, before being called to education. Along the way, she has also gained an MBA and a PhD in social sciences.

Mabel is the founder of the Liberty International Christian Organisation - a charity founded in 2007, helping the distressed, disadvantaged and disconnected use knowledge of spiritual laws and principles to heal from emotional traumas of the past and rebuild their lives to become whole, harmonious, self-reliant and independent. Many have achieved this goal.

Mabel regards herself as an educator whose passion is helping others to use their talents and natural abilities to discover and pursue their life purpose unto wholeness and happiness.

The mockingbird -
a symbol of harmless innocence, mimicry and music

"If you just learn a single trick, Scout,"
like improving your attitude,
"you'll get along a lot better with all kinds of folks."
Atticus Finch

Contents

"A person may have all the culture that modern civilisation can provide;
and may have a string of degrees after his or her name, a yard long;
and may be the most skilled person in his or her chosen field,
but if he or she carries around a bad mental attitude,
that person will be a failure,
as surely as two and two make four.
The one thing people will not tolerate is a negative mental attitude."

Andrew Carnegie

Preface

This book is the result of three decades of observing, studying and interacting with people in counselling, researching and teaching. The climax of this experience is in working with the emotionally challenged, who were abused, betrayed, disconnected, unloved, rejected and disempowered. Consequently, they went through life with a negative attitude, wondering why they could not get along with other people. They come from all walks of life and different ethnic groups, communities and nations. You can find them as neighbours, co-workers and colleagues. We may hear their cries as distant echoes in far-flung areas and dismiss them as irrelevant until we too are forced to walk in their shoes.

Some people do the things others do and get different results. Why? Attitude may be the reason. We don't often appreciate the consequences and impact of negative attitude on our lives. Observers note that 80% of success in life is based on attitude, while 20% is a result of gift, skills and knowledge. We live in a cruel world, the poet Richard Gallienne says, "For the world is given over to the cruel sons of Cain." Therefore, society is made up of people hurting people through hatred, criticisms, judgemental attitude, jealousy, envy, put-downs and resentment. Thus, people, as friends, family, co-workers or acquaintances become the source of our discontent.

But we need people. Otto von Bismarck observed that "plans only succeed through people." Tony Blair said "people are our masters." They are "a source of power," noted Lord Scarman, even though our disputes come from them. What is society but a group of people, interconnected and interrelated? The ability to deal with people is a valuable skill. Therefore, we are encouraged to become devotees of the doctrine of getting along with people. This calls for an appropriate pleasing attitude.

We all have unmet needs. They result from the pain and hurts of the past, pressures, challenges and anxieties of the present and unfulfilled dreams. These needs are our lack. "All our lack is people-based," writes Oral Roberts. For example, if you lack time, you are struggling with demands made on you by yourself and others. If you are lonely, you lack loving friends or family relationships. If you lack peace, you are in a negative relationship causing strife, conflict, arguments or resentment. Thus, all our unmet needs emanate from people and can be solved through people if only we inculcate the right attitude in getting along with others.

During the research to conduct, refine and perfect the attitude questionnaire used in this book we were amazed at the enormity of the problem facing people. Of those interviewed, 40% disliked people. Therefore, they avoided them or were indifferent to them. George Bernard Shaw calls indifference "the worst sin against our fellow creature and the essence of inhumanity." Some of those who avoided others are traders and storekeepers! If you dislike and avoid people, how can you build rapport, bond with or sell to them? You cannot learn or accept anything from them. Worse still, you cannot value, appreciate, trust or relate to them. Therefore, the more we understand other people's attitude, the better we can get along with them.

There are many books on the power of positive attitude, but very few on other forms of attitude. This book seeks to readdress the balance. The book discusses ten attitude types between the positive and negative poles. There is a lemon test to compare your present attitude with those surveyed and a 21 days programme to help you ditch negative attitude and replace it with a more appropriate pleasing one.

It is a book of self-discovery and self-help. In it you will discover your dominant attitude, its origin, unintended consequences and impact on your life. You will also discover the obstacles that have held you back until now and understand other people's attitude and their stance. The book is offered as a tool. You can use it for reflection and self-analysis to clarify your feelings, choices and their consequences to date. Then you can decide to weed out wrong negative attitude and break free from ugly past experience, failures, fears, unwanted memories and contrary ideas. This will make room for you to inculcate a more appropriate attitude through change, effort and patient persistence. You are in control and you have the prerogative to change for the better, free from arguments, strife, conflicts, contention and unhappiness.

Einstein defined Insanity as "doing the same thing over and over again and expecting different results." But the willingness to change for the better shows wisdom and maturity. This author used the principles in this book to change her impatient attitude to a better one. Many of those counselled also used it to change their wrong attitude and are living better lives today. You owe it to yourself to have a more pleasing attitude that enables you to get along with people and achieve what you want through them.

Chapter 1
Introduction

A gentle answer turns away wrath [displeasure or indignation]
But harsh words stir up anger

King Solomon (Proverbs 15:1)

We have all witnessed and observed them from a distance; ugly scenes of angry people shouting at each other. Shoppers mingled with irate people, cussing and verbally abusing others. There is resistance, disagreement and disrespect. The peace of the area is shattered and we stand aloof watching as people dishonour themselves. Why do respectable-looking people do such things? Inappropriate attitude is often the answer. Attitude is the major cause of antagonism, strife, conflict, disagreements, quarrelling, raised voices, altercation, discord and non-cooperation.

Many who are ill-equipped with people skills interact and try to get their way. They fail to honour and respect one another. One is discourteous without meaning to and the other responds adversely. Both trying to get their needs met from a position of pain, pressure and hurt from past experience. Result? Deadlock! Unmet needs.

If only we can learn to speak softly, to placate others instead of antagonising them, to request instead of rebutting and demanding, to compromise instead of complaining and commanding others, we will get our needs met. I have watched customers walk into a store and demand certain things that are unheard of and expect instant service. For example, an American friend came to visit me in London. She wanted some cereal that I know is only available over there. She insisted on the attendant locating this particular cereal for her. When the girl look puzzled, my friend became impatient. When it was explained to her that the particular cereal is not available here, she asked why not? Now I am sure that she was not trying to be difficult, but she still had her mind focused in the United States, instead of London. An ugly scene could have arisen if either of them had been the shouting type. We apologised to the pleasant attendant and left the store.

Sometimes, patients in hospitals shout and demand instant services. Hospitals operate in ways they find works for them. For example, a patient may have waited all day for his surgery but because of emergency operations that day, the theatres are busy and they cannot operate on him. Sometimes he is in pain, but does not say so or ask for pain relief. He may have already determined the date and time of his discharge. He wants to attend to other plans, which he does not wish to cancel. He makes unreasonable demands. The staff members try to explain the unfortunate situation and apologise for the delay. But often the patient will have none of it. He becomes impatient to have his surgery. The relatives join in to demand their rights. What more can the attending staff do? There is misunderstanding, conflict and anger, all because people cannot get their way.

To those who are easily angered, Solomon says "Do not be easily provoked in your spirit, for anger resides in the lap of fools" (Ecclesiastes 7:9). Not many will regard themselves as fools, yet they easily resort to anger and make unreasonable demands. As one shop assistant said, "It is not the demand that irks people, but the way they are made." Often the one making the demand looks down on the attendant.

Some people turn up their noses in a demeanour of derision to demand things from others. They have already lost the game, for the demeaned will react if burdened with the experience of being put down. If mature, she will smile nicely and serve the high-minded and eventually disarm him. Often attendants are ill-trained and ill-equipped to deal with insults. So the customer feels insulted for having to wait to be served. Many will demand to see the manager and complain. But a little exercise of patience would have seen both parties satisfied.

I remember incidents during my research into the consequences of support services outsourcing to private contractors. The private contractors employed foreign girls who could not speak English, but were determined to learn and keep their jobs. The in-house services employed "pillars of the establishment" on their staff. Results showed that the foreign girls served all customers joyfully with pleasing attitude, no matter the circumstances. The more some patients insulted them, the broader their smile. Probably because they did not always understand the nuances of insults couched in pleasant words. But even if they did, the girls were determined to keep their jobs by giving good service. In the end their pleasant attitude won the day. They helped to elevate the support services to a professional status and changed its menial face forever, such is the role of attractive personality and pleasing attitude.

From other studies, we find that lack of appropriate attitude in dealing with others results in disagreement, conflict and discord. Yes we hurt, yes we have been abused, yes we want instant service and we must get our way or no way. But if the attitude we employ is counterproductive, all we get is discord and anger. When we change the manner of approach, peace and gladness reign and both parties are satisfied. Sellers get repeat orders, patronage and no ugly scenes, while customers get their needs met. Appropriate attitude is always the answer, not anger.

Chapter 2
What is attitude?

Aptitude may lift you high,
but only the right attitude will keep you there

Attitude is defined as a settled way of thinking, feeling and behaving towards things, circumstances or people. It shows up in your thought patterns, the way you speak, your tone of voice and in what you say. Your body language and mood - whether cold or warm - are determined by, and reflect your attitude.

Attitude is also a choice you make and a way of life that becomes a lifestyle. Every day, there are people and things to upset you, but you can choose to smile instead of frown through them. You can choose to be glad instead of sad, to love in place of hatred and to be benevolent to others instead of mean. First you choose your attitude and then work to attain the goal as a lifestyle. As Ralph Marston said, "Excellence is not a skill. It is an attitude." No one was born being excellent or a failure, but as you make a choice, you work towards it as a goal until you achieve it.

Attitude is also a mindset, character, personality and the image you present to the world. These are discussed on the following pages.

Attitude is a mindset

As a man thinketh in his heart, so is he

James Allen

The heart and mind are used interchangeably. You are a spirit, you have a soul, made up of your mind, will, emotions and imagination, and you live in a physical body. You relate to people and the world through your soul. Your thought, reason, emotion, character and personality are attempts of your inner spirit relating to the world.

Attitude then is your mindset or belief system. It reflects how you associate idea; the things you observe, concentrate on and pay attention to. It dictates what you care about, how you judge people and things, the decisions you make and how you arrive at them. All these are reflections of your mind and thought processes.

Your belief is your reality. Whatever you believe becomes your unshakeable reality. It does not matter whether the belief is right or wrong, as long as you believe it, you will think, act and conduct your life in accordance with the set of principles that govern that belief system. Your beliefs can become a stronghold in your mind. No one can bring you out of that stronghold but yourself. You have the key. The key is changing the way you think and deciding to come out. Thus, your attitude is the totality of your beliefs, which are subject to change.

Many people seem to learn from their personal experience, but wise people learn from the experiences of others and use it to improve themselves. Why reinvent the wheel? "As you continue to think, so you will remain," says James Allen. If you think you can, you will. If you don't think you can, you won't. Whatever you think and believe, you will feel, talk, walk, look and act, according to your thoughts. You will also attract and hang out with similar people. This is the law of attraction. We attract what we focus on and what we feel within. If you think you are ugly and don't like yourself, you will attract similar people. Misery likes company.

From our attitude survey, 4% of the people surveyed disliked themselves, 23% said they only fairly liked who they are, while 73% were happy with all that they are. Thus, 27% of people disrespected and dishonoured who they are and devalued themselves so their self-esteem plummeted. But, as Anthony Trollope advised, "Never think that you are not good enough...people will take you very much at your own reckoning." Unfortunately, many people think that they are unlovable or worthless, and so remain. So think and value yourself.

Your attitude or mindset will dictate your lifestyle. It is a posture of how things stand with you in your personal world. Successful people tend to be more optimistic. They learned from the school of life to be hopeful, unlike some negative people. For example, some abused women expect men to abuse them. It is a mental stronghold.

A lady, we will call her Anne, was physically and emotionally abused and traumatised. She was helped to clean herself up and reconnect. She finally got married to a very nice gentleman. However, she still expected the husband to abuse and beat her. When he would not, she goaded and baited him. When he refused to accept the bait, she called him names and thought that he was not man enough. It took therapy, counselling and healing to change her mindset. Now that she is free from her mental stronghold, she accepts that not all men are abusive. You too can be set free from your erroneous mindset. Thus, attitude as mindset is your standpoint in life. It can be a milestone to grind you down or polish you up for all that you desire and aspire to in life. You become that which you think and believe.

Attitude is character

"It is not difficult for a person to be polite in words and courteous in actions to individuals who are classed in the same social scale or who, perhaps, are above him in wealth and influence. The test of a true lady or gentleman comes when that individual is brought in contact with some one who is considered beneath her or him, some one who is ignorant or poor."

Booker T Washington

Character is the totality of who you really are when alone, when there is no mask, no façade and no image management to impress anyone. It is your consciousness. Attitude will reflect this inner you that is your character, the essence of who you are. It is your modus operandi, the way you conduct your life, business, manage your affairs and respond to challenges, crisis, circumstances, setbacks and people. Thus, your attitude to life reflects and becomes your true character in words and conduct.

In life people may beat you up, pass you up or pick you up; it all depends on your response to the hand life deals you. Winners and losers respond differently to problems, opportunities, challenges and people. Winners see every challenge as opportunity for change and improvement. They decide promptly. They don't dither and wait until all the conditions are in their favour. They show worthy character. But losers exhibit a negative attitude that drains them of energy. They end up whining, complaining, blaming and sometimes insulting everyone but themselves. Remember the support services workers; the people they served saw them as menial labourers to be insulted and demeaned. They saw themselves as service givers, grateful to have the opportunity to serve the sick and helpless. Their interaction was a testament to their individual attitude and hence character. They responded differently because their characters, as attitude, were significantly different.

If life hands you a lemon, don't spend the rest of your life complaining about it. Squeeze the lemon. You may enjoy doing it and find that the lemon is more than just a sour fruit. But until you decide to do something with the lemon, you will never find out. You can choose how to respond to every situation you encounter and your response will reflect your character or attitude and determine whether you succeed or fail.

Character is built and sustained by trust, cooperation and the humility to esteem and celebrate others without demeaning yourself, the consistency of being predictable and the endurance to stay the course. Character is also measured by honesty, confidence and courage to live by the truth even when you stand alone. For "the strongest man in the world is he who stands alone," said Ibsen, when he stands for what is right and just.

We find that most people don't progress or succeed because they are plagued by inconsistency and lack of endurance or persistence. They are tearful one day and boisterous another. Some are confident and bold one day and fearful wimps another. They start a project and give up halfway. By their attitude they are not dependable, trustworthy or loyal to employers, family and friends. This is a character flaw that is reflected in their relationships as bad attitude. Consequently, many make no progress in life and cannot be employed for long. But flawed character can be rebuilt and attitude changed or improved.

Many people do not spend time building a worthy character. Therefore, they exhibit wrong inappropriate attitude. Some unfortunate ladies we encounter in our charity have been so traumatised by abuse, hatred and rejection that they have not had the time to live, let alone build their character. Therefore, they exhibit inappropriate attitude. It is one of blame, fear of rejection, lack of initiative, energy and willingness to start and complete anything. But it is never late to start and engage in character building to improve attitude. Many are improving and some have gone on to change their attitude for the better. You can never rise higher than your character. You cannot build a worthy character without the right mental attitude. Therefore, when you change your attitude, your character will change.

Attitude is contagious. As iron sharpens iron, so people of appropriate attitude or character will influence to sharpen and impact those they come in contact with. Attitude as character is the melting pot of issues, determinant of ultimate destiny or achievement of purpose. For character is destiny. Thus, attitude as character can contaminate, pollute or purify and mould those its possessor relates to. For example, the educator, Booker T. Washington, states that he learned more from people of integrity he encountered in his life than all the books he read at college. Character is caught and transferred more by association than learning from afar. Furthermore, people will rather employ and train a less skilled and competent person with a good pleasant attitude than a highly qualified person with the wrong attitude. Thus, attitude can become a potent tiebreaker between people in employment decisions.

Attitude is personality

To see ourselves as others see us is a most salutary gift
Aldous Huxley

Your personality is what you seem to be to onlookers and acquaintances alike. Attitude will reflect your inherited mood. It may be bleak and gloomy, or bright and happy. Until you change it, your mood will remain and colour all that you do in life. Some people are diffident, reserved and introverted. Others are fearless and daring. Some are belligerent and bold, while others are subtly domineering and controlling. Some are boisterous and bold, while others seem shy and docile, or loud and proud. Inherited personality is not etched in stone; if it is not serving you, change it for a more appropriate attitude for your need. Many people live under a façade, image managing their lives. Our survey reveals that 5% of participants dislike hypocrisy or pretence in people. Such personality and character are incongruent and false.

Attitude reflects your posture in life. It is expressed in a high moral tone you use or the coquettish way you behave. Attitude is hubris. It is the self-confidence and boldness to assert yourself and get things done a certain way. It is the audacity to be who you choose to be without apologies or explanations as personality approximates to character and you become the same in private and public life.

Furthermore, attitude as personality is a choice you make. You can choose a negative or a positive one, or any in-between shades to suit your need. Attitude is also learned and can be unlearned. So if your present attitude is not working for you, you can change it. Attitude is irrespective of the circumstances you find yourself in or how others choose to treat you because it comes from within you. It is your choice. As Saint Augustine said, "Happiness is related to the condition of the soul and not bodily well-being or wealth." Right attitude expressed in personality can enhance, to lift you up to a desired altitude in life becoming a stepping stone for all you desire.

It can be a springboard for promotion or a pit of hell that shackles you to unending rounds of disagreements, strife and conflict in dead end relationship, or jobs you cannot escape from. Even when promoted, if your attitude is not right, hence your personality pleasing, the position attained will not last and you will crash down even lower than before. Attitude as a pleasing personality is the essential key to success in life and without it goals are not easily achieved through people.

Attitude is image

We are all in the gutter,
but some of us are looking at the stars
Oscar Wilde

We live in a world of opinions. Within ten seconds of meeting someone, we form an opinion as to their economic status, education, level of confidence and credibility. Rightly or wrongly, this impression or opinion determines how we interact with them. Image is how others see you before you have a chance to speak. If the image they perceive is not friendly, open and attractive, in other words, if it is odious, repulsive or antagonistic, you have already built a barrier to interaction. You cannot connect with others. They feel uncomfortable interacting with you. You have lost before you start.

In the social world we live in, we can send congruent message to others in order to be perceived right. These messages of attraction or repulsion are sent through:

- The clothes you wear
- The demeanour in which you conduct your life
- Gestures
- Manners
- Body language
- Words you say

People first notice your clothing. Do they fit and are they in the right combination of colours or not? Are they clean and in good repair? Or soiled and worn? They observe your deportment, the way you carry yourself. Are you smiling, inviting and open? Or frowning? A smile says three things to a stranger: "You are important to me. I want to be your friend. I want to be of service to you." You cannot be smiling and frowning at the same time. You cannot be smiling and be sad, sullen and sour at the same time. Most people are put off by the vacant withering stare of the indifferent. Your face mirrors your soul for others to see.

The confidence in your step determines your inner spirit and mood. Are you fearful, shy and gloomy, or happy, self-assured and bold? Are your steps deliberate and even, or hesitant and sluggish? It reveals your level of self-control, or lack of it. Thus, your attitude, hence image, will be reflected in how you carry and conduct yourself. We may all be struggling and suffering from past experiences, but some choose to walk tall on the inside by improving their attitude, hence image.

During our attitude questionnaire studies, we met a lot of people. We noted how some were inviting, approachable and very helpful, while a few were indifferent, self-absorbed, unhelpful and sometimes repulsive. It is a shame because we are all interconnected. Everyone has something you may need or learn. If you cannot connect with them, how are you going to get it?

Your body language speaks volumes. Sometimes people say one thing and express another by their body language. This is the mixed message of the insincere. It is a wrong attitude that repels others. Of our respondents, 5% called it hypocrisy. The more attention you pay to your image, the less you have to worry about convincing others about your integrity, trustworthiness, openness and authenticity.

The aim of right attitude is to put others at ease, make them comfortable and helpful for mutual benefit. As you attract others by being open and friendly, you build rapport with them and they are enabled to help you solve your problems. For example, many patients in hospitals complain and criticise those who care for them. Therefore, they build barriers to having their needs met. When some realise the error of their ways, they change, heal faster and go home to their comforts.

One such patient we will call Charles. He had a near fatal accident and was paralysed. He could do nothing for himself. When he came to us, he was depressed and saddened by his injuries and became self-absorbed. He could not connect with those caring for him and got nowhere with them. Everyone expected him to die. As the days went by, he realised his predicament and decided to change his sullen, uncooperative attitude to one of gratitude. Even though he could not communicate verbally, he could smile and use his eyes. He started smiling at the therapists and nurses. Soon, everyone took more interest in him and his condition began to improve. Even his relatives become less critical of his care and started helping instead of hindering those caring for him. By a small change in his attitude from uncooperative sour and grumpy to one of gratitude and friendship, he started to improve, recovered and went home. The healing power comes from within. It is the spirit of man that sustains him in sickness. A sour uncooperative spirit or attitude is not conducive to healing and health.

From this and similar cases, the law of expectation asserts that:

> When you expect the best in everything and everyone, you reflect the same attitude in your conduct, and the best in everything and everyone will be attracted to aid you achieve your desire.

Perhaps those who feel unloved and unlovable should reflect and obey this law. Similarly, the law of attraction states that "you attract what you are." Like attracts like. So if you are helpful and happy, you will attract similar people to help you. The reverse is also true.

The words you continually say have an effect on your life. Nature grants you whatever you say. Those who continually grumble and complain curse themselves unawares. They suffer the consequences of their words. We hear people saying they are "dying to do something" or their "feet are killing them." They curse themselves. Words have power and we eat the fruits of our words. The power of life and death is in the tongue. Worse still, people curse others with words and adversely mark them for life.

Many emotionally challenged people we see were inadvertently cursed in childhood. They have carried the burden through life and are marked by them. Consequently, they have a beaten down image or attitude to life. Until they lay down the burden of the past, they get nowhere. Those who cut the ties with their ugly past have improved their attitude and image, and healed. You can do the same to improve your image.

Therefore, your attitude is the mental image you have of yourself. If you think you are worthless, unimportant and a victim of circumstances, that is how the world will perceive and treat you. Until you change this mental concept of yourself, nothing will change. We all hurt in different areas, but we must find better ways to heal.

Your character is your attitude. If you spend time building a worthy character of hope, honesty, integrity, dependability and sincerity, others will trust you, connect and be more comfortable interacting with you for mutual benefit.

Your personality is not set in stone. If you inherited a gloomy, fearful, docile or sour, domineering and controlling disposition, work to change it and build yourself a more pleasing personality, and so improve your attitude.

Finally, your attitude is the image you present to the world. People will form opinions and impressions about you based on what they see. We live in a critical and opinionated world. Have a pleasing, open, friendly and helpful image that puts others at ease and makes them comfortable in cooperating with you to meet your needs.

The home - where we can go as we are and be accepted without question, is also where beliefs, habits and character are formed and nurtured for life

Chapter 3
Shapers of attitude

As the twig is bent, so grows the tree

The home and the social environment that surrounds us are the two dominant shapers of our attitude. However, education, work environment, associations, traditions and experiences determine our choices and self-concept that also help to shape and manifest the attitude others see.

We interact with the environment through our five senses of hearing, sight, taste, feeling and smell. We are influenced by the media, music, movies, soap operas, the internet and books. The people we interact with also influence us. Because people do what they see others do, we pick up on habits, foibles and manner of speech, and make them our own.

In the present age of peer pressure and role models, it is easy to inculcate the habit of peers and role models into our daily lives. Thus it becomes more profitable and helpful to imitate positive and beneficial attitude and leave the negative and destructive ones alone because as the child is bent in childhood, the adult will grow. For example, we discerned that most of the troubles and travails of the disconnected, disadvantaged, abused and rejected that we help started at an early age. They were marked by life before leaving home.

They were unaware of the source of their trouble, while some remained in denial. However, through counselling and interaction, their attitude or character improved, through introspection, self-analysis, acceptance, change and sheer hard work, they healed. You can do the same.

The external environment, people, and early life shape our attitude. Eight shapers of attitude are discussed below. This is not an exhaustive list; readers can add to it from their own experience.

The shapers of attitude are:

1. Family upbringing
2. The environment
3. Education
4. Experience
5. Traditions
6. Choices
7. Knowledge of the Word
8. Self-concept

Family upbringing

Family life is a potent shaper of attitude. What is formed at an early age remains with many people into adult life and marks to either make or break them. We inherit the genes of our parents and absorb all that we see and observe in childhood. Like a sponge, we soak up everything and grow to be like our parents. If you are brought up in a family where negativity is rife, you will grow up negative in outlook because you know no alternative. Thus, your personality and character are formed at an early age. We established above that your attitude reflects both your personality and character. Researchers have proven that by the age of 5 years, 82% of character or attitude is formed. The gloomy, controlling, fearful and easily angered may be formed at home. Thus, adult life becomes a period of refining inherited attitude to an appropriate one.

Your belief system

Your belief system is shaped at home. Whatever your parents believe in, you will tend to believe. If you are brought up in a Christian home, you will become a Christian early in life, and if brought up in a Muslim home you will tend to be a Muslim. Thus, your concept of belief systems is shaped at home in childhood and adolescence.

Some of our ladies were told by well-meaning but misguided relatives that they would never amount to anything and they believed it. Others were told that they were useless, unworthy, worthless and had blanks for brains. They believed all that because they had no alternative views. Thus, they grew up handicapped by the word they heard and believed. They felt, acted, walked, talked, spoke and behaved in a manner consistent with all they heard and believed. They are not alone. This is the tragedy of most of our upbringing. Unfortunately, we can believe anything, true or false. Until we know better, the erroneous remains.

Science is a case in point. Not long ago, many believed that the world was flat until proven otherwise. At the advent of the computer, some believed that they fouled things up. Sydney Brenner, the scientist, said "The modern computer hover between the obsolescent and nonexistent." Now we know better and some work exclusively from their computers.

Some people grew up with misconceptions and distorted mindsets. In cultures where males are pampered and served, they grow up thinking that women were created to be handmaidens for their every need. In other cultures, some girls regard men as "dogs" because that is how they were presented. This mindset is difficult to adjust in adult relationships. How can one relate to someone they believe is a dog?

Sibling rivalry

Parents have the arduous job of loving and treating all their children the same without favouritism. Where siblings perceive that one child is favoured above others, rivalry ensues. Healthy rivalry can be outgrown, unhealthy is toxic, deadly and competitive. For example, biblical Isaac loved Esau, the outdoor son who could bring home the venison game he loved. But wife Rebecca loved the quiet, stay-at-home Jacob. Esau got his father's love, leaving Jacob resentful of the love denied to him, resulting in toxic competitive rivalry. Jacob supplanted Esau, trading his brother's inheritance over a bowl of stew in a moment of extreme hunger. Later he got the blessing and became a fugitive. Esau became a restless wanderer, bitter, angry, purposeless and vowing to kill his brother (Genesis 27-28:1-9). Their descendants are still at enmity today!

One generation later, history repeats itself. Same Jacob loved Joseph, son of his old age, more than his brothers. The brothers resented his favoured position and hated Joseph. They could have killed him, but by God's grace, sold him into slavery. Favouritism births jealousy and envy. Jealousy is a possessive distrustful spirit that wants to keep others down and within sight so they cannot get ahead or escape.

Envy is a selfish, greedy spirit that wants to have what others have, but because it cannot, it is consumed with insatiable craving and ambition for alternatives. But envy and jealousy can spur on competitive spirit for growth and development. As Solomon said, "All achievement springs from a man's envy of his neighbour." However, toxic envy and jealousy breed hatred, resentment, covetousness, competition and selfish craving for alternatives. Thus, toxic sibling rivalry can shape attitudes into bitterness, hatred and anger, leading to deadly competition for alternatives.

Some older siblings, by culture, appoint themselves chairpersons of the board, ruling others with an iron fist. They intimidate, terrorise and criticise the younger ones until some become timid and fearful. As elders, they may assign and delegate duties to their siblings in an attempt to keep them down. These overbearing ones learn their trade at home and over time become very bossy and insufferable in nature and dictatorial in attitude. Some carry this bad attitude into relationships in adult life and wonder why others cannot tolerate them at home, work and in business or marriage.

The younger siblings resent their domineering attitude and grow up nursing inferiority complexes. Some unfortunate ladies we counsel spent their lives serving their elders in the belief that the elders will in return care for them. Unfortunately, their beliefs were unfounded. They realised too late that those they trusted and served were all the time indifferent to their welfare. They felt betrayed, used, abused and became suspicious of all others. It has been difficult for them to relate to others due to past experiences. These inferiority complexes can play havoc in latter years.

Some who were dominated, intimidated or constantly threatened at home to obey became insecure and fearful of authority and unable to take responsibility for their actions or initiate anything in case they fail. They resent all authority and may grow up as people-pleasers. Their gifts, creativity and imagination were smothered and dampened early in life, so they often hide behind routines. Their attitude is often protective against blame, criticism, discord or argument, and they cannot say no. Thus, the fearful and insecure nature of adult life may have been bred at home.

Interestingly, some people are more respectful, appreciative and patient to friends than siblings or mates. They value their opinions more than family members or mates. Perhaps these people suffered a wounded spirit or broken will at an early age to make them submissive. In adulthood, they turn the opposite way. As Booker T. Washington observed, "By nature, people react to painful experiences by swinging like pendulums to the opposite direction." They lost the will to fight their corner at home and want nothing more to do with such people. Thus, they may accept what life and people dish out to them because there is no fight left in them.

Some people feel unloved and unaccepted by parents and siblings. They grow bitter and insecure. Some are alienated and orphaned. They go through life with an orphan spirit of rejection, abandonment and destitution looking for love in wrong places to compensate for what they think they missed at home. Some try too hard to be accepted and loved by those they encounter, mostly mates. Perhaps because they try so hard while inwardly fearing rejection and abandonment, they attract what they feel within, rather than what they desire. Some end up in gangs or unhealthy cliques.

Many become distracted by the search for acceptance or love, and miss opportunities or possibilities that can enhance their character and panache to make them the hunted, rather than the hunter for affection. Fear can also keep some from relating to others, and when they do some are too dependent, clinging or possessive.

The orphan spirit is not only suffered by the unloved and unaccepted. We live in a society where absentee fatherhood is the norm and single mothers try to raise sons without experience or help. These boys grow into men only to wonder who they are. Whose son they are and what is their role in life without a role model? Many are very angry, bitter, insecure and fearful. The emotional scar of an absentee father leaves them vulnerable, inadequate and handicapped.

Some resort to pursuit of personal accomplishment or bravado to compensate for their emotional bankruptcy. When "things" pursued don't fill the void within, their anger explodes. There are core values only a father can give a man. A man gets his sense of identity from his father. Where this is absent, men become vulnerable to repeat the mistakes and become absentee fathers too. They are emotionally distant and unengaged in relationships. Adult relationships without skills become a problem. Their mates, who don't really understand their silent emotional stance, wade in to fix them or to convince them that all is well. Some ladies blame themselves for their spouse's emotional turmoil and disengagement. Drama ensues, misunderstanding is rife. They blame, criticise, argue and disagree, ending in discord. Thus, many adult relationship problems can be traced to wrong attitude shaped by emotional trauma during childhood at home.

The abused

These are a special group. They were abused by relatives at an early age. They grow bitter, hating the likes of those who abused or refused to protect them. Their attitude in later life becomes resentful, bitter and angry. Some of them vow to have nothing to do with the gender of their abusers. Until they lay down the past through genuine forgiveness, they are unable to heal. Because you cannot put new wine into old wine bottles, they cannot make new relationships work until they are free from the old, abusive and traumatic ones. Children from abusive homes tend to abuse others. Hurting people hurt others. Therefore, these people go on to abuse others and the cycle continues for generations. This scenario is exemplified by those we counsel. Many are healed and some are making progress. Forgiveness is the key to healing. The prisoner you set free from the past is yourself. Until you do, freedom and liberty remain elusive.

It is also interesting that some people attach different meaning to childhood experiences of seeming abuse and trauma and are not marred by them while many are. Our threshold for pain, abuse and degradation differ, hence the meaning we tend to attach to experiences and their aftermath in adult life.

But families are not all the same. In many families, children feel accepted, loved and protected. They grow up well-adjusted, ready to go out and make indelible marks or change the world. Even boys raised by single mothers can adjust well and learn their manly roles wherever they can. There are many notable orphans, like Nelson Mandela and Andrew Jackson, who become world leaders. Others, like Louis Armstrong and Johann Sebastian Bach, made their marks in music. Hence being an orphan is not the issue. The meaning of the experience makes the difference.

Some abused, rejected and unloved people grow up to forgive their parents and relatives by choice. They forget the past, lay down all its ugly, negative baggage and build new lives of hope, right attitude and freedom. Thus, family upbringing is a major shaper of attitude. Early life may mark you, but you can overcome and become who you want to be. As Carter Godwin Woodson said, "All that is worthy for anyone, he must work out and conquer for himself."

The environment

The social environment includes homes, schools, colleges, playgrounds, recreation centres and workplaces. Anywhere you spend time with friends, mates and other people will influence your attitude. Bad company corrupts just as iron sharpens iron. The company you keep, choices you make and interaction with those you encounter will shape your outlook on life. Friends may advice to influence your attitude, but you must use wisdom to conduct your life aright.

Indeed we draw materials, images and words from the environment to build our thoughts. These thoughts form ideas and are acted out. The thoughts and actions repeated over time form our habits. Habits crystallise and become set like cement into strongholds that are very difficult to break. Thus, our habits are influenced and formed from the external environment we live in, whether for good or bad. These habits then manifest as attitude.

As you grow up, certain self-images may become appealing. You will choose the image you want to portray to outsiders. You will speak, act and conduct your life in accordance with your chosen image. Thus, the social environment in which you live, work, play and encounter people contributes to shape your attitude.

Educational level

As you progress through higher education, you may leave home and become responsible for your life. You may be influenced to change certain mannerisms, and hence your attitude. The influence may come from mates, peers, reading or studies. You can improve yourself, develop in certain areas and become mature in others. Thus, the level of education, the lessons you learn and choose to incorporate into your life can influence your attitude through better choices, decision-making, and the degree of open-mindedness to change and adapt to others.

Many people's lives were framed by the characters of those they encountered at educational institutions. Booker T. Washington notes that, "There is no education which one can get from books and costly apparatus that is equal to that which can be gotten from contact with great men and women". His life was marked for good by his teachers and he grew up from slavery to become a world changer in his day.

Similarly, some of my most memorable and character forming occasions were times spent with my mother and my teacher, Mrs Edna Whitehouse. Between them, they marked and moulded me into all that I am today.

Education per se does not shape your attitude, but all other factors combined and your willingness to change by inculcating what you learn. Consequently, some educated people have negative fixed attitude, while the uneducated may be more pleasing, flexible and harmonious in attitude. That's life.

Life experience

Experience is another potent influencer and shaper of attitude. Many people face crisis that form their mindsets for life. An ugly, traumatic or emotional experience can mark and change your attitude for life. Your mindset can be chained to an emotional experience that becomes a mental stronghold. Until you decide to free yourself from this stronghold, nothing else in your life will be meaningful. For example, some of our ladies were dominated, put down and made to feel worthless by their spouses. They vowed never to remarry after their divorce. Some who were trapped in these dreadful unions were rescued by Providence. They all needed to heal from their experiences before they could meaningfully relate to others. I am glad to say that many have.

If you try things and fail you may become sad, discouraged and disillusioned. Without help and encouragement, you may quit and refuse to try again. In time you can become pessimistic, gloomy, cynical, suspicious and distrustful of everyone and everything. But if you succeed often, you may become optimistic and upbeat, with a fearless, cheerful attitude towards life and future challenges. Thus, the challenges, obstacles and crises you experience in life and how you respond to overcome them will shape your attitude towards pessimism, hatred or optimism and forgiveness in future. Simply putting your past life experiences have a potent influence on your attitude.

Traditions of men

Many live in societies they did not choose. By birth, force or circumstances, some find themselves in cultures and customs not of their own making. The prevailing traditions set by forefathers are not inherently wrong, but may not suit present needs. Traditions like dress codes, gender issues, lifestyles, educational levels and acceptable manner of speech for individuals can be determined by local culture and traditions. In certain cultures, machismo is the accepted order. In such places, women are regarded as handmaidens, there to serve and not to be loved, accepted or valued. Tradition can help or hinder progress. Thus, attitude is shaped by customs, cultures and traditions.

Choices we make

Man is a free moral agent. The power of agency is that we can choose how to conduct our lives. Since we are responsible and in control of our choices, we must bear any unintended consequences and enjoy ensuing benefits. Many choose to live behind a façade of bravado or flamboyance and flattery.

Others may choose a more sedate, confident or people-pleasing attitude. Each may succeed in the short term, but eventually their attitude will be seen for what it is. If false, the consequence will be exposure and shame. If real, time will prove them honest people of integrity. From our survey, 5% complained of other people's hypocrisy, selfishness and pretence. Some ladies choose their mates against better judgment, even when the handwriting is on the wall to the contrary. They complain when what could be discerned earlier comes home to roost. Some think erroneously that they can change others. We are only responsible for ourselves. However, we must not allow grievances or sufferings from our choices to overshadow subsequent opportunities that could be deliverance from bad choices. Freedom of choice negates cause to blame others or to complain.

Knowledge of the Word

Christians, who walk by faith and not by sight or the five senses, have the word of God as their mantra and book of conduct. They choose to see challenges through the promises of God. They have unshakable trust in God because He is faithful and not fickle or changeable like man. They also believe His word implicitly, because God and His word are the same. Therefore, they are more hopeful and confident, and less anxious, fearful and worried than others. This is faith-living.

The confidence Christians have is based on the unconditional, enduring love of God. He so loved the world that He gave up His only Son to save and recover the world from Adam's fall. The born-again Christian is forgiven of all past mistakes and sin, reconciled and at peace with God, redeemed or purchased back from Satan's hold, loved, accepted and adopted into God's family forever. A child of God will never be rejected, abandoned or betrayed by Him. God is the perfect Father who provides for every need of His children, protects, preserves, guards and guides them into His perfect pre-ordained will and destiny. Consequently, there is no cause for fear, worry or anxiety when faced with challenges or trials. The victory is already decided in their favour. They only need to suit up, boot up, show up and stand firm to experience the deliverance of a loving Father. This is the experience of mature confident Christians.

Maturing Christians, however, are still renewing their minds on the word and promises of God in order to understand who they are in Christ. Therefore, they are at different levels of character (attitude) development. The Christian identity self-image and self-esteem are in Christ. Their confidence is in His finished work. Your identity is who you think you are. Self-image is how you think, conduct and carry yourself. Your self-esteem is how you love, respect, honour and value all that you are.

Christians are hidden in and robed with Christ, they bear and should portray His image and glory and should exhibit His attitude. But because of the levels of maturity, many Christians are working on their attitude (character) like everyone else. Many feel unloved, undervalued and unaccepted because they have not accepted the free, unconditional unending love of God in Christ. They are emotionally empty and expecting the love of man to fill the void they feel. But as Augustine said, "Our hearts are restless until they rest in you." God created the human heart for Himself, to fill it with His love. Until we accept this, we will feel unloved, unfulfilled and empty within, exhibiting inappropriate attitude like some maturing Christians.

Some Christians with negative attitude were marked by family upbringing, customs and traditions. Some were told that they will never amount to anything in life and they believed it. Many were abused, maligned or mistreated by people they trusted. Some suffered the orphan spirit or are still living in the past, resentful, bitter, angry and scared, needing emotional healing and freedom from mental strongholds.

However the attitude you present to the world is how the world will see and treat you. When you change your attitude the world around you will also change to accommodate you. No one wants to be around negative people. They contaminate and make you gloomy and sad. Life is sad and gloomy without burden of negativity. Thus, it is not faith alone based on the word of God you know that shapes your attitude, but all the other shapers of attitude combined determine the ultimate attitude.

Self-perception

This is the way you think and see yourself from within. Therefore, you conduct your life and carry yourself accordingly. It may be framed by all or some of the above shapers of attitude. It may also be a result of words you chose to listen to. As these negative words ring in your ears, you internalise and believe them. They become your reality.

If you perceive yourself as ugly, useless, hopeless, clumsy and worthless, that is the image you will present to the world and that is how people will regard and treat you. Most of the negative thoughts and beliefs are self-fulfilling prophecies. Those who fear rejection and refuse to risk relationships, when they do relate, they are rejected. Whatever you fear within, you will attract. It is a universal law. Therefore, change the thoughts about yourself, your perception and conduct will change. Your attitude will be reflected in your new conduct as you carry yourself differently. Thus, the way you see and value yourself within is how others will see and treat you.

Eight shapers of attitude are discussed on the previous pages. Whatever areas or mixture of areas that influenced to shape your attitude to life, it is hoped that you can reflect on these and be willing to improve your attitude for better harmonious relationships.

The Eagle -
A symbol of courage, keen focus and freedom.

The attitude to be and soar above the constraints
and confines of conflict and confusion.

Chapter 4
Types of attitude

The unexamined life is not worth living

Socrates

The types of attitude people display are as diverse as there are people on earth. Metaphors of birds are used to depict the different ten attitude types discussed below in accordance with their manifested dominant nature. The different types range in a continuum from the positive to the negative. Each has its own beauty, benefits and burdens or consequences.

The essence is to reflect on your own dominant attitude. We are eclectic by nature. We pick up bits and pieces from all types and make them our own. But there is one that dominates. Focus on that one, refine it or exchange it for a better one.

Types of attitude

- Positive attitude of the golden eagle
- Negative attitude of the hawk
- Pitiful, victim attitude of the nightingale
- Fearful attitude of the ostrich
- Fearless attitude of the mockingbird
- Blasé attitude of the peacock and parrot

- Beaten attitude of the mournful dove
- Commandant attitude of the rooster
- Caring attitude of the hen
- Critical attitude of the carrion crow

Positive attitude [Golden Eagle]

The ultimate mark of a person is what he or she does in times of challenges and crises not in comfort and convenience.

Positive attitude is a "can do" attitude of champions. This is the attitude to be. It is a prerequisite for success and personal achievement that enables its possessor to soar, like an eagle, beyond natural ability. It is a winning attitude, full of hope.

Purposeful living

Possessors of this attitude focus on their life purpose. Of the participants in our survey, 51% said they have a life purpose. With a definite purpose and plan to achieve it, positive mental attitude will give power to thought and enable realisation of objective. Thus, purpose can birth great achievement through positive mental attitude. These eagles are motivated, passionate and enthusiastic. They enjoy the galvanising power of inner forces that the pursuit of purpose provides. They are self-disciplined and determined to achieve their destiny and channel their effort in that direction.

Purposeless living

Of the people surveyed, 49% had no purpose in life. Without purpose, we tend to drift, focus and dwell on the ephemeral and fickle, rather than the eternal and fulfilling. Emotions are unbridled and feelings rule us. Without direction to channel effort, the purposeless may crave substitutes like being completed by others. The lack of wilful pursuit attracts distraction. Life becomes indeterminate emotion-charged and volatile. People become rootless and helpless. Purpose is God-given and ordained. Until you find and pursue your purpose, very little in your life will work as desired. But when in your purpose, all that you desire will be added to you. Relationships, joy and the peace you crave and hanker after will manifest as God makes your enemies and critics to live at peace with you. Your flare and panache will shine through as fulfilment comes. Therefore, get a purpose to die for and watch all else being added to you as icing.

Reaction to challenges, risk and change

The people who exhibit this attitude welcome and thrive on challenges they regard as opportunity for change and progress. Therefore, they take calculated risks and initiate action. They are creative thinkers who let their imagination roam for innovation. They are disciplined, self-controlled, patient, well-rounded, and balanced. For them, change is inevitable and continuous. As Heraclitus said, "It is in changing that things find purpose." The purposeful are in all works of life as janitors, judges, ministers, musicians, artists, engineers and entrepreneurs. Once they take flight, nothing stands to hinder them.

Personal attribute

These are people of character; they are dependable, honest, predictable, consistent, loyal, trustworthy and yet very humble. They are givers and go-getters, sacrificial not selfish, compassionate not condemning, helpful and generous, with their time and resources in grooming and developing others. They are self-confident, self-reliant people of vision, courage and initiative. They are emotionally controlled extra milers.

They know who they are and love all that they are. They value, honour, accept and esteem all that they are. They are happy and contented people, not intimidated by competition, opposition or people. Their lives have meaning. They believe in themselves and expect favourable outcomes in all they do. Some are perfectionists, flawless in performance, turning others off. Their optimistic and stress-free life can improve their immune system and longevity. Their healthy outlook in life is full of fun, energy and vitality. Thus, they may be keep-fit and health food enthusiasts.

They forged their character through struggles, sacrifices and concentrated effort on what is important to them in the school of life. They are persistent people of endurance. Stephen Mansfield tells how Booker T. Washington tried to produce the best brick at the Tuskegee Institute, in Alabama, where he was the principal. He was determined to produce the best, but getting the kiln to cooperate was another matter. After the third kiln collapsed, many teachers and students gave up on the project. Washington was not deterred. He was going to produce the best brick, or die trying. He went to town, pawned his gold watch to purchase the best kiln at the time and success was achieved. This is the spirit of excellence that refuses to cut corners to produce shoddy work due to lack of funds or pressures. It is leadership by example. He stood knee-deep in the mud until the job was done. It is as Winston Churchill said, "Victory at all costs, victory in spite of all terror, victory however long and hard the road may be, for without victory there is no survival." Successive students and teachers reap the benefit of his hard work. Thus, these eagles are generation builders who easily attract to influence and impact the lives of friends, colleagues and others.

Similarly, when Frederick Douglass wanted to escape from slavery, he prayed for deliverance. He said, "I prayed for twenty years but received no answer until I prayed with my legs." He took the initiative to deliver himself. He risked death, by drowning and bullets, but persevered until he escaped to freedom on his third attempt. He went on to become one of America's eloquent orators, spokesman and a brilliant writer. He could have remained at his post, suffering, whining and complaining, but through sheer force of character (attitude), he overcame all the obstacles that beset him and made a name for himself. Through determination and attitude, you can do the same.

Reaction to people

These people love to interact with others. They have learnt the secret of getting the most out of people through cooperative endeavours. They are like Charles Schwab, who assumed great responsibility in helping Andrew Carnegie create great wealth and in so doing earned the right to great riches himself. They cooperate with others for mutual benefit. They always expect good in and from others. Their expectation taps into the deep well of potential within them. As deep calls to deep, they help to bring out the best in others and help them soar. Some manage others and channel corporate effort towards successful enterprises that would not be possible without their personal attribute, vision and willingness to assume great responsibilities. Consequently, many of them become corporate builders and leave worthy legacies.

Chapter 5
Negative attitude [Hawk]

Every frustrating and enfeebling situation that has
threatened to shrink and limit me has served to broaden
my scope and to enlarge my soul

King David (Psalm 4)

This is the mother of all negative attitudes. It is the melting pot of negativity, boasting of all that is ugly, defeating and unproductive. It is the exact opposite of its positive counterpart and the attitude not to be. It is defined as a contrary, judgemental, cynical stance of bitter and defeated individuals. It mires people in anger and bitterness from past experience to preclude success and negate personal achievements.

The bitter has abrogated every inalienable right of liberty and the pursuit of happiness and embraced a self-imposed prison cage of bondage and unhappiness. The dungeon of the past in all its ugliness has eclipsed the present and future leaving only a bucket of ashes on the cold stone floor to plague the mind. This is the attitude of the abused, betrayed, maligned, subjugated, scarred, wounded, and oppressed, who arise from their degradation, hovering like the hawk, to get even. Anger, hatred, bitterness, resentment and unforgiveness are its hallmark.

The hawk hovering over its domain seeking prey to devourer

Purposeful living

Possessors of this attitude do not engage in a meaningful purpose in life. As Stephen Mansfield said, "Without purpose one loses the galvanising power of inner forces that purpose provides." Therefore they glide through life, like the hawk, seeking prey to devourer. They have no goals or plans. Daily life becomes a meaningless existence. Some may choose revenge as their purpose, seeking prey, unhappy, complaining. They focus on schemes or plots to pay back their tormentors, measure for measure. Their hatred can manifest as physical illness needing medical treatment. Their aim in life is to settle accounts with those who hurt them. Consequently, most issues of life are either neglected or put on the back burner. This is the spirit of Biblical Esau, who despised his birthright and, in a moment of hunger, sold it for a bowl of stew only to blame his brother for deceiving him and taking away his blessing (Genesis 27:1-40). Later he "pursued his brother, Jacob, with a sword stifling all compassion because his anger raged continually and his fury flamed unchecked" (Amos 1:11).

Reaction to challenges, risk and change

When faced with challenges and problems, they engage in a war of attrition with authorities and departments. They don't submit to anyone's authority, but would rather argue their case, even when they are wrong. They blame everyone for their plight and refuse to take responsibility for their actions. From our research, many people in dire straights blame the Government, relatives, school system, fate and God for all their hardship and suffering, yet do nothing to remedy their situation.

They disapprove of every risk as harmful, costly, dicey and inexpedient for them. However, if they can scheme to defraud and dispossess another, they would engage in dubious ventures for personal gain. When faced with change, they prefer the status quo, convenience and security without complexity and uncertainty. Thus, they are risk-averse, like the 73% participants in our study, and resistant to change, except for personal gratification.

Personal attributes

These "hawks" lack self-confidence and don't seem to appreciate who they are, like the 27% of people surveyed. Because they spend valuable time scheming and plotting revenge, they have no time to plan for success and personal achievement. Therefore, they are often intimidated by others. They resent their self-imposed feeling of less than, and lash out at those who make them feel small. For example, when some faith people were heard confessing that they were "blessed beyond measure," those with negative attitude were "ticked off." They cannot stand anyone feeling "better than." But these people were only "calling those things that are not as though they were." Like Abram, whom God renamed Abraham, "father of multitude" when he was childless. Eventually, he confessed his name long enough to become what he said. But the "hawks" will have none of it and resent any "intimidation" from anyone.

Most of them don't know who they are, like the 27% of people surveyed. They dislike their lot in life and wish to change places with the "successful." Because they cannot, they envy and hate them with passion. They blame them for standing in their way of personal achievement! As Booker T. Washington writes, "People react to painful experiences by swinging like pendulums to the opposite extreme. If humiliated and subjected, they will emerge from their degradation bent on pride and fame." Consequently, possessors of this attitude, having suffered in the past, have chosen to remain in the past, but to gain fame and fortune to compensate them for their lack of success. They plan, scheme and plot deceptive ways to achieve their plans. They slander to shame and discredit their nearest and dearest and sometimes to defraud them.

They harbour treacherous thoughts against others and conspire to bring them down. For example, the story is told of family meetings where certain issues were agreed upon and everyone present signed in agreement. The negatively inclined went ahead and unilaterally did their thing, contrary to what was agreed. When asked why, they simply said, "They changed their minds." Many months later, when their actions rebounded on them, they blamed it on the organisers of the meeting!

This is the hallmark of this attitude. They feign friendship and agreement, while inwardly they are deceptive, sly and slippery in their duplicity. They will slander and subvert to supplant and supersede others. Like Biblical Absalom against his father David, they wish to usurp other's position and hard work (see 2 Samuel 15-18). Many are insincere and cannot be trusted. Consequently, many people avoid them.

Some find ways to cause discord and separate happy family members, friends and other household members. For example, we saw an auntie who decided that none of her family members was going to live in peace because of what "they did to her." She set out to sow seeds of discord between fathers and sons, mothers and daughters, and between sisters. When the family members realised their plight, they quickly made peace with one another and ostracised her from their midst. Thus, many are deceptive, divisive and destructive. They were hurt and they go on hurting others.

At work they want to wield authority but loathe submitting to one. Productivity is delayed and progress grinds to a halt as subordinates keep their distance to avoid arguments. As friends they can be self-seeking, inflexible, disagreeable and bossy. Unfortunately, some also resent their plight but do nothing to change their attitude.

Reaction to people

Because they don't value or appreciate who they are, they cannot value, like or appreciate others. They are intimidated by others' presence. They feel less than, and insecure. Therefore, they lash out at anyone they think is superior to them. With toxic tongues, they mercilessly shoot caustic words like bullets at others. All interactions become discordant and result in disagreement and strife. They judge, criticise and seem never to forgive minor offences. As Mother Teresa said, "If you judge people, you have no time to love them." For example, we had a lady who brought a notebook where she recorded all that her family members did to her over forty years! She carried her little black book around and referred to it at every conceivable moment. Whatever happened to filial love, affection and forgiveness, we asked?

Some are oversensitive and moody. Relating to them is like "walking on egg shells." You have to mind every word you say in case you offend and upset them. Hence many avoid them like the plague.

Unfortunately possessors of this attitude have not allowed the enfeebling experiences they suffered to enlarge their scope for compassion towards others. Instead, they let their past shrink and limit them with negative attitude and lacklustre existence of hatred, bitterness, envy and unforgiveness. As Edmund Burke said, "All men that are ruined, are ruined on the side of their natural propensities." They refuse to forgo anger, bitterness and hatred to forgive others and are ruined by hatred. The irony is that the success they crave in others can be attained with effort. But because they detest it in others, they "attract what they are within and not what they desire," according to James Allen. We cannot contravene the laws of nature with impunity.

In certain cases, the object of their hatred and anger is long dead and gone, but still the fury of hatred rages because to them their pain was never acknowledged or validated. They walk about with a permanent scowl on their faces, hating and being hated in return. Somehow many of them flock together and can easily recognise themselves in a crowd. They share their plight, plan and scheme their revenge and buddy together in a form of "brotherhood or sisterhood" of the wounded and grieved.

Many of them don't realise the nature of their attitude. Only those around them can know the misery and pain they create. They deserve our prayers for meaningful change. Many are lonely because of their attitude towards those who care for them. Their pain and bitterness have become mental strongholds, deep-rooted, embedded and fixed like the sycamore trees. But genuine forgiveness can release them from their self-imposed prisons and dungeons.

As Richard Lovelace said, "Stone walls do not a prison make, nor iron bars a cage," but the bitter in attitude has created own prison dungeon and chosen to live in it instead of taking the high road of forgiveness unto happiness and freedom from pain and bitterness.

But they have a choice to change like everyone else or remain mired in pain and bitterness blaming others for their predicament. They can use the power of their choice to forgive all their prisoners including themselves and be set free from the dungeon of unhappiness.

Some older ones have seen the error of their ways and changed to attract new friends. They now appreciate the difference a change of attitude and flexibility in thought and action can make to their daily lives.

"I know why the caged bird sings"
Maya Angelou

*"A bird doesn't sing because it has an answer
It sings because it has a song"*
Chinese Proverb

"We think caged birds sing, when indeed they cry"
John Webster

Chapter 6
Pitiful, victim attitude [Nightingale]

By nature all men are alike.
Through practice they have become far apart

Confucius

This is the "woe is me" victim type of attitude. It sings nightly of its woes and victim status as the eternal victim of Fate and circumstances. By day, it springs into action. The attitude is defined as a manipulative, attention-seeking stance of the selfish.

Purposeful living

Possessors of this attitude have carved out a life purpose of being the centre of attention. Their goal in life is to have attendants running around them supplying every need and pampering every whim. Therefore, they focus on getting what they want and woe betide all else. Life and success is measured by the degree of attention.

Reaction to challenges, risk and change

When faced with problems or challenges, they dump them on any available person and forget about them. Even those known to be incapable are burdened with jobs and assignments they cannot possibly carry out. When failure comes as expected, they blame and ostracise the unfortunate ones. They have no risks to bear and can easily blame those they depend on for any misdeeds. They never take responsibility for anything. Blame is their trademark. Many of them always come out smelling like roses, no matter the occasion, for nothing is ever their fault.

Personal attributes

Personally they like their indolent life of ease. If married, husbands become errand boys in the proverbial "honey do" state. He is endeared with honey and sent to do all that needs doing all in the same breath. Some are quite capable but refuse to lift a finger, complacent while others toil. For example, there was a friend who was always either on the verge of dying or at death's door. She never worked and did no housework. She managed to give birth to two children and retired from life. So her husband had "three children" to mind, as well as go to work, earn a living and attend to all the housework.

Unfortunately, one day her husband had a heart attack and died after a week. The day after his burial, she got dressed and began to face life and the reality of her situation. Since then, she has never complained of any ill health or impending doom. This may be an isolated case, but such is the power of life crisis to cure instantly what years of pandering and attendance were unable to improve.

Usually, some have a history of abandonment or lack of acceptance. They decide to become the hub of the wheel of life and have others circling their pivotal persons. Anyone who refuses to circle around them is deemed insensitive, uncaring and inconsiderate. When they don't get their way, they resort to temper tantrums like two year olds. It is ugly to see adults behaving like babies, as seen on tennis courts.

Some have expansive and selective minds that can magnify misery or feign imminent death in order to attract the attention they crave. As patients, they can be very difficult to manage because you can never be sure when they are craving attention and when they really feel as bad as they make out, despite all the evidence to the contrary.

They may look the epitome of good health, yet are on the verge of a terrible disorder. They are always the first on the healing lines but never seem to get healed. The song, "Nobody knows the trouble I've seen" seems to be written for them.

Reaction to people

As co-workers, they shirk work and complain that "their feet are killing them" or "their backs have given way." Everything they do must be dramatic and hyped to the limit. As subordinates, they are nowhere to be found around their posts, let alone delegate duties to them. They feign helplessness. Some manage to ingratiate themselves with the boss and spend valuable time tale bearing and gossiping as people-pleasers, telling others what they want to hear and so avoid doing their duty. Misery loves company and many find it with like-minded people to pity-party.

As bosses, they cannot maintain order because they are lazy, preferring to recount their woes rather than work, hence those under them do likewise. As friends, you must pander to their every whim or you are not a good, caring friend. Life is all about them. They are selfish and self-centred in their nature and manage to sap other people's life and energy. Thus, their relationship with others must be about them or none at all. Many become the proverbial "drama queens and kings." Fortunately some have realised that none was born a victim as Bishop T.D Jakes writes, "Forever a victim? I don't think so." Furthermore, as Robert Greene said, "These incurably unhappy and discontent are often unstable in character and have intense emotions. They may present as victims of Fate making it impossible to see their miseries as self-inflicted. Those who rush to aid them may be sucked into a whirlpool contagion by association." Thus some people are enticed to help them only to be afflicted and suffer. Many have learnt to beware!

Many have been shaken into reality by crises and were forced to change. It is interesting that many people trapped in loveless and controlling relationships don't consider themselves as "victims."

Many have realised the unhelpful nature of their lifestyle through friends and therapy, and changed. Therefore, change is possible. Old wounds can be healed. Pain of abandonment does not have to swing like a pendulum into self-centred selfishness and indolent complacency, which are the hallmarks of this attitude.

Fearful ostrich, unaware of its surroundings

"The lion creates no gaps in his way - his movements are too swift,
his jaws too quick and powerful.
The timid hare will do anything to escape danger,
but in its haste to retreat and flee,
it backs into traps and hops smack into its enemy's jaws."

Robert Greene

Chapter 7
Fearful attitude [Ostrich]

No human passion so effectively robs the mind of all its power of reasoning and acting as fear

Edmund Burke

Those medically diagnosed and treated for phobias were excluded from this study. Fear is a basic human emotion designed to protect us from harm and danger from the external environment. However, some people have adopted a fearful attitude as a way of life. They fear going out and fear staying in. They fear poverty and fear riches. Some fear work and fear idleness. Some fear dying but talk incessantly about doom, gloom, sickness, disease, getting old and death most of the time. They fear daylight and fear darkness. Many fear success and failure. There is no limit to the diversity of fears that grip the mind of the fearful. A few with fearful attitude may also become diagnosed and labelled with phobias. Thus, they are marked and stigmatised for life.

Purposeful living

Possessors of this unfortunate attitude are paralysed and crippled by fear. Their life purpose is handicapped and any goals they manage to set are derailed by fear. They arrange something today and cancel it tomorrow. Indecisive and insecure, they can muddle through achieving very little because the mind is gripped with fear of failure.

They fear starting anything in case it fails and fear finishing anything in case it does not work out. Therefore they become overcautious, risk averse cowards. At the first sign of trouble, threat or challenge, they hide like the ostrich and hope that it will blow over. Some take flight or fight with all their verbal know-how. They lack initiative and ambition. They prefer to accept defeat without protest and sometimes without trying because they fear criticism. They are quitters at the first huddle. Because they quit, they become failures. They loathe taking responsibility for actions and blame others if it fails. They prefer others to make decisions for them for the same reasons.

Personal attributes

Personally, some are timid in nature, awkward and nervous with strangers. They lack poise and pride in who they are. They have low self-esteem and lack self-confidence. Their outlook is always bleak, anticipating the worst. Their best of times are also their worst of times!

Some tend to agree easily with others' opinions to avoid argument, discord or confrontation. Many suffer from inferiority complexes and become rather verbose in expression as a cover-up. Few people have a brazen façade to hide their fearful nature. Many are overanxious or worry a lot. They procrastinate and prevaricate ad infinitum, ad nauseam and get nothing done.

Sometimes they compromise easily to their own detriment. Unfortunately, it is established that whatever holds you down in life will continue to do so until you actively deal with it. People repeat their mistakes because they refuse to learn from them. As George Santayana noted, "Those who cannot remember the past are condemned to repeat it." The fearful remembers the terrible past experience that let in the spirit of fear and paralysis. They are just unwilling to confront their demons. For example, some ladies fear betrayal, loss or failure so they don't get involved in meaningful relationships. Yet they yearn for husbands and families of their own. The contradiction between desire and attitude makes realisation unattainable. Thus, many become lonely and unfulfilled and later in life, regret years wasted in fearful attitude.

Some are trapped in unhealthy, abusive and belittling relationships but cannot take the initiative to improve or assert who they are, to change their situation and end their hurt and misery, so they suffer in silence and do nothing.

As leaders they often doubt others' ability to do their jobs well, hence they over-manage and over-supervise others offloading their fears and anxiety on them. They remember all those who tried and failed, but never those that succeeded. They spend their lives planning for failure, instead of success. They seem to know all the roads to disasters, but not how to plan and avoid them. Because they entertain fear, a negative emotion; other fears like poverty, ill health, loss and infirmity, crowd in.

As a result of their inner fear and worry, they tend to attract people of similar attitude and wallow in self-deprecation, condemnation and guilt. Their inherent fear, worry and constant anxiety lead to stress that begets indigestion, poor health and insomnia. This self-deprecating attitude and condemnation means that in time they become what they constantly focus on as fears become self-fulfilling prophecies.

Reaction with people

In their relationship with others, irrational fears, muddled thinking and inability to keep up with routine work can subject them to being the butt of friends' jokes. Fears and suspicion of others make them vulnerable and sends mixed messages to others. However, many people encountered during research are compassionate and helpful to the less fortunate. In spite of the mixed messages sent, the fearful are helped and accommodated. The hallmarks of this attitude are indecision, procrastination, lack of initiative and inaction.

Chapter 8
Fearless attitude [Mockingbird]

The righteous are as bold as a lion

Proverbs 28:1

The righteous are those who base their life, boldness and trust on God's faithfulness because they are in right standing with Him. Therefore, they are fearless in attitude. Fearlessness does not mean unmitigated gall of the arrogant, irresponsible and haughty. Fearless here means the courage to dare and the confidence to step out in faith knowing that the whole resources of heaven are at your disposal. This is the stance of a mature Christian walking by faith and love where quitting is not an option.

Purposeful living

Possessors of this attitude have a preordained purpose and calling. Some were set apart from birth, like the prophet Jeremiah of old, for a mission. Consequently, they have a predetermined destination and focus on their set plans to achieve their goal. They are people on a mission and live purpose driven lives to achieve their destiny. For them, constancy of purpose is a lifestyle.

Reaction to challenge, risks and change

When faced with challenges and problems, they already know the expected outcome as good, whatever the result. Like King David before them, they know that "every trial or frustrating situation is in reality a divinely given opportunity to overcome adversity by fully utilizing one's talent and ability." Therefore, they work within the opportunity offered to learn, grow and develop. This equips them for future trials and tests. They commune with their God and employer to seek direction, guidance and grace for whatever life brings their way. They are people of reflection, thought and imagination.

Personal attributes

Personally, they are self-confident based on the faithfulness, power and mercy of their employer. They esteem and value all that they are because they are needed and helpful for their assignment. They have a servant heart that is other-centred. These are great men and women, like Oral Roberts, Charles Stanley, Billy Graham, Kenneth Copeland, Smith Wigglesworth, Kenneth E. Hagin, John Osteen and many more who served and are still serving from a sacrificial heart of love and compassion for others. Their great achievements are monuments to God's glory and the grace available to believers.

These generals of God's army have personal issues, but they pale in significance to the attitude of hope and faith with which they face life. They are people of character, trusted in public and private, untainted by scandal. They have integrity, honesty, faith, courage, commitment to their calling, loyalty, consistency, endurance and patience to develop worthy leaders, mentor and add value to others for memorable legacies.

They were not born with character, but struggled and developed the attitude needed for their mission. Above all, they are people of great humility devoted to their God and people. They forged their character (attitude) in solitude and manifested it in service for great success. You too can work on your attitude (character) and develop it. As Albert Einstein said "A weakness of attitude becomes a weakness of character."

Reaction to people

Their relationship with people is based on their calling. To be ambassadors of Christ in healing and helping hurting humanity and the saints know and experience the unconditional love and boundless grace of God as Father, provider and protector. They interact with passion, enthusiasm and above all compassion for everyone. They motivate and encourage others, tirelessly discharging their duty to bless generations of people. I am a beneficiary of their energy and work through partnership and thank God for their lives.

The uninitiated may regard the boldness and courage of these public servants of repute as hubris. There is a fine line between arrogance and boldness. If you knew that your plan could not fail, you too will be fearless in its execution. That's perhaps the basis for their fearlessness. The servant heart of the preordained and called negates arrogance and pride otherwise failure is sure to follow. However, some of them endure a lot of criticisms, jealousy and envy bordering on hatred, from those unaware of their purpose, assignment and mission or indeed the life that they have to live to achieve what they have. Perhaps, as King David said, their "boldness and courage can magnify other people's cowardice and complacency to cause conflict." But through it all they stand fearless, because they are divinely upheld and sustained to achieve their mission in life. Like the mockingbird, they can fight their corner.

Those who know and embrace their life purpose can achieve similar success and personal achievements like these giants. If you want what the fearless, bold and successful has, then do what they did to attain it and you will have the same. The hallmark of this attitude is unwavering faith in God's faithfulness and mercy.

"It is not only fine feathers that make fine birds"

Aesop

"I know of only one bird - the Parrot - that talks;
And it can't fly very high"

Wilbur Wright

Chapter 9
Blasé attitude [Peacock or Parrot]

A person's desires determines his way of living
King David (Psalm 10:5)

This is the carefree attitude of the fun-lover. Whatever is not fun is not for the blasé. They desire and demand fun at work, play, relationship and association, or not at all. The attitude is defined as an emotionally charged stance driven by desire and joviality. Possessors of this attitude are found in all works of life. Some are so laid-back they are almost horizontal. They are casual and offhand in their remarks and nonchalant in nature. Consequently, many regard them as uncaring to their plight.

Purposeful living

Many are purposeful, focused and determined in pursuit of their goals. There are more fun-lovers than are serious. These have not yet found their life purpose. When faced with challenges, the blasé can jest through it all and come out still smelling like roses. They are risk takers and eternal optimists who succeed often.

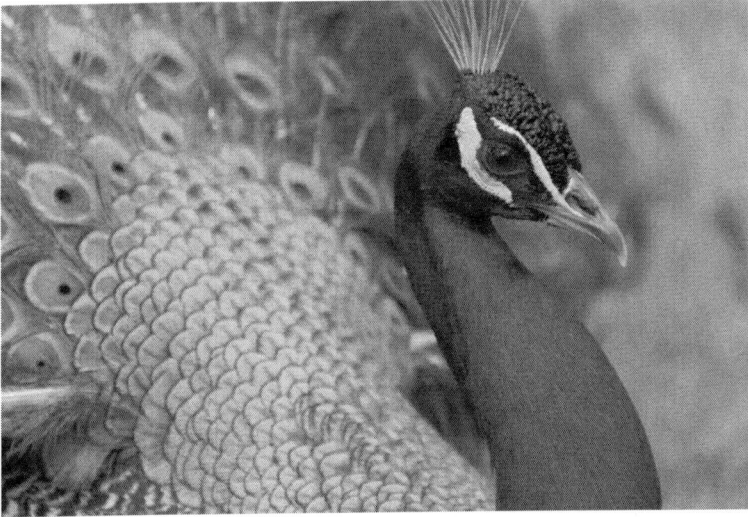

Personal attributes

Personally, they are self-confident and hopeful of favourable outcome provided it would be fun. The less serious among them are loud and talk incessantly about the self and fun to be enjoyed. They jest and joke, sometimes inappropriately. They can be disloyal, unreliable and difficult to cope with if duty conflicts with plans for fun. Sometimes the blasé attitude can be adopted to cover up fear-based insecurity and timidity. Where such is the case, other signs of cowardice and indecision will surface for accurate discernment of innate attitude from the adopted one.

The blasé attitude can also be a competitive ploy to cover up shrewdness in business. Many of them succeed in business as entrepreneurs and artists because their creativity, roaming imagination, productivity and carefree nature are not stifled and constrained by bureaucratic routines. Many engage in publicity, promotion and customer services simply to be seen and noticed.

However, some are low achievers because they spend so much time having fun and partying that they leave other things, even preparing for examinations, to the last minute. Consequently, many engage in part-time work that allows them free time.

They dress in flamboyant distinctive ways, some with the gypsy look, loudly coloured fancy hairstyles and beautiful designer jeans with distinctive emblems or marks, unusual accessories and make-up that make a statement wherever they are.

Some sport tattoos and body piercings. Many are looked upon as peacocks because of their distinctive outfits and fun-loving lifestyle, but they are mostly not arrogant, only different and blasé. The Parrots among them are very clever, colourful in outlook and make their marks as designers, artists, cartoonists and illustrators. They have energy and disarm others with their infectious laughter. They dislike silence and love music. Their spontaneity to celebration is contagious. No one has to invite them to a party.

But some get into debt to fund their distinctive tastes. Some may drift into substance abuse and get on the slippery slope to crime and violence to fund their unique lifestyle.

Reaction to people

They relate very well with people. They make good associates and friends with the fearful to lessen the dread and doom that beset those. As co-workers they help lighten the mood and atmosphere of drudgery and routine, and can lift morale during sad and difficult times. But they are great encouragers and motivators. Some in authority find it difficult to maintain order because they are rather frivolous at times and their friendship knows no boundaries. Consequently, they end up as second in command. The hallmark of this attitude is fun-loving and distinctiveness.

Chapter 10
Beaten attitude [Mournful Dove]

When you control a man's thinking,
you do not have to worry about his actions

Carter Godwin Woodson

These are the people who have been conditioned to think that they will never amount to anything in life. That they have blanks for brain and are useless, clumsy and no amount of education and struggle will change their condition, and they believed it. They have tried a few things with that mindset and failed a few times and have given up the fight. But as Abraham Lincoln writes, "Failing is not the end until you quit trying."

Some possessors of this attitude have accepted abject poverty as their bane in life. Some bear wounded, scared spirit or broken will. They were dominated, oppressed, alienated, unaccepted and traumatised by chronic fault-finding in high-control homes. They despair of life and find no strength in trying anything anymore. Discouragement and disillusionment have given birth to hopelessness and sorrow. They wallow in a beaten-down, worn-out attitude, resigned to anything life hands out. They become indifferent to the world around them. They groan and shuffle under the weight of their degradation. George Eliot's "frozen stare of indifference and despair" is the hallmark of possessors of this attitude.

Purposeful living

Many have no set purpose because they cannot face trying anything. They "know it will be hopeless to even try." Consequently, life is lived from day to day. Some have crawled up into their beds refusing to undertake activities of daily living. Their sorrow and melancholy deaden them to pain. They have resigned from life waiting for death. But death does not come to those wishing it.

Reaction to challenges, risk and change

Most people with this attitude from our studies are poor and have accepted poverty as a way of life. Therefore, they have abdicated from challenges. They say they have nothing to risk. They accept whatever decisions others make on their behalf. Many are overcautious, always waiting for all the conditions to be favourable. They waver and procrastinate. They worry about uncertainties and are gripped with indecision. For many, nothing changes until their mental stronghold of poverty and futility are dealt with. Some have renewed their minds and gone on to try again and succeeded. For example, a lady who was on welfare renewed her mind on poverty and got off benefits. She now works like everyone else and takes responsibility for her life.

Personal attributes

Those broken by abject poverty cannot find the courage to go on. They have no confidence until they change their mindset. Many are physically bowed down, weary and unable to straighten up because they bear their troubles of universal proportions like Atlas. They are hopeless and helpless, needing care, compassion and mercy. They mournfully display their sorrow and the sadness of their plight for all to see.

Some were rejected, criticised and subjected to misery or were made to feel less than their siblings at an early age. Many are in unhealthy loveless relationships. They carry their pain, shame and sorrow into adult life expecting no different from others and the world. They are the real victims of society. Some are so dejected, overwhelmed by misery, grief and wretchedness that their misery and shame become contagious. Many would-be restorers and helpers may avoid them.

Fortunately, many found renewed hope from the testimony of others and decided to try again. For those who accept this second chance, as soon as their attitude to life and living changed, they got a new lease of life and went on to achieve the dreams they let die and the hopes they abandoned.

For those still wallowing in misery of past humiliation and defeat, I say arise and try again. Failing is halfway to succeeding. Only actions you take now can get the results you desire. You cannot change your past, but you can use the present.

Remember the story of Sparky, who flunked all subjects at school? He was timid and had no friends, because no one appreciated him. However, he loved to draw and when he submitted his art work and drawings, they were rejected. But he did not quit. He continued to draw and sent his drawings to studio after studio until he wrote his autobiography in cartoons. The final ensuing popularity of his cartoons led to countless books and films. Finally the world took notice of a Mr. Nobody who refused to quit. My friend Sparky was better known as Charles Schultz, the creator of Peanut comic strips characterised by Charlie Brown. He failed at many things and could have had a depressed, beaten down attitude to life but chose to rise up on the inside and use his talent to reach others and in reaching them, he succeeded.

You have not tried enough times to give up the fight. Imagine the inventors of our times if they had given up after a few trials and quit. Where will the discovery of the incandescent light bulb be? Thomas Alva Edison tried 999 times before he succeeded. He went on to become the invention wizard of Menlo Park with more patents to his name than any other.

Many other unsung heroes have been beaten down and maligned by others but they rose up, dusted themselves down and began again. Perseverance brought them success because they refused to quit. For example, an unknown Norwegian had very little education and so could not find jobs. He even went to America twice for jobs and only managed to work as a streetcar attendant. Even then he was never good at it because he was always scribbling in his notebook. Finally he had enough; jobless, hopeless and hungry, he went back to Norway. He put his scribbling together and someone edited and published it for him. He won the Nobel Price for Literature in 1920 with "Growth of the soil," a story of his beaten down life. He was Knut Hamsun.

Abraham Lincoln failed at business and attempts to enter the United States Senate, Legislature and Presidency for over 30 years before he finally made it to the White House. Where there is a will, a winning attitude resides to lift the defeated to greater heights than would have been possible without failing. If life hands you only lemons, don't cry about it, but find a way to squeeze your lemons and make lemonade. Some people may buy it and make you rich. You can forget your woes and shame. Therefore, my beaten down, dispirited friend devoid of will power, arise and the sun of new beginning may just shine upon you to smile again. As Art Williams writes, "Life will hand you whatever you will accept." Be it poverty, riches, degradation or success.

Reaction to people

We met few people with this attitude on our survey. They simply stared at us wondering if we came from another planet to bother them. It was disconcerting and pitiful. Most of them don't connect easily with people, having become self-absorbed and mostly indifferent to all around. Their docile bodies and enfeebled state arouse compassion. They are not disabled, yet weaker and more infirm than the physically disabled. Crippled by imagined fear of poverty and abject poverty, they cower and shuffle away from others feeling inferior, even from those not their equal in character or ability. This is the tragedy of fear-based or real poverty. George Bernard Shaw called poverty "the greatest evil and worst crime." He advised all to sacrifice all else and resolve not to be poor. He realised the enormity of loneliness that results from being beaten and feeling inferior. As Horace said, "Do not despair." Arise and try again.

Those in unhealthy controlling relationships fear consequences of their action. In cultures where women are beaten for wrong expected behaviour, they may suffer in silence. Some seek healing help covertly. Some pursue illusionary distractions of redecorations, holidays and meaningless diversions to ease their pain or misery. Thus, the mournful dove seeks love, affection and self-fulfilment to fill inner void.

Chapter 11
Commandant attitude [Rooster]

The greater the power, the more dangerous the abuse
Edmund Burke

These are the eternal godfathers or godmothers, forever in charge and in control by self-appointment. They put themselves up for election, appoint themselves and become tyrants. Then they unleash their oppression and tyranny to abuse those they profess to rule. The hallmark of this attitude is absolute domination and control. Unfortunately, power is never total. As Anthony Giddens said, "Oppressed subordinates have countervailing power to resist oppression and subjugation."

Purposeful living

Possessors of this attitude elect to rule and reign over all they come in contact with. This is their purpose, dream and desire. Control is the goal and power is the route. Those who refuse to be dominated and abused are criticised and ostracised. No ethnic group or culture is immune from this attitude. We only have to search the annals of history to unravel the atrocities committed by others in the name of slavery. The recent case of a slave turned "male companion" being beaten to death in a hotel room in London, is a case in point.

Reaction to challenges, risk and change

Possessors of this attitude are fearless in the face of challenge. They wield authority like a staff and command everyone into action. They delegate what they cannot do and expect instant favourable results. They take uncalculated risks and blame others for failure. Change is constant with them provided others labour for it. However, they are self-seeking and self-serving. Whatever the change, it must be for their personal benefit or they will rule against it, condemn it or ensure it never takes off. Thus, their selfishness, fear and deep insecurity make them uncooperative and disagreeable.

The Rooster rules the roost

Personal attribute

Possessors of this attitude are overconfident of their power and status, demanding complete control and total loyalty from all who serve them. They answer to no one and are unwilling to submit to authority. They dictate and expect obedience. They are detractors of every good ideas or plans that do not come from them. The world must revolve around their interests or stand still. They are authoritative, bossy, commanding, controlling and domineering in nature. If they are not in charge, they will not get involved. Even in areas where they are least competent, they still try to dominate and tell the experts what to do and how to do it in a macho way. They stifle creativity and innovation from others.

They give subordinates just enough room to do routine things they dictate and direct from above. They act like lone rangers, founders of corporations who try to run them like private businesses. Some may have succeeded in certain areas, but they try to extrapolate their success into every arena of life without adaptation.

As family heads, they rule with iron fists to feather their own nests. They assign menial duties they are not willing to do to others. If anyone tries to reason with them, they claim insubordination. For example, the story is told of a family of two brothers. The younger went away to find his fame and fortune. Having made some money, he went home to his elder brother to help raise him up from poverty and improve their family. He had to be rescued from his ancestral home as the elder brother tried to annihilate him for coming to show him up as unsuccessful and impoverished. He was the eldest and if anything was going to be done around there, it would be done through him as the one in charge. As David said, perhaps this was a case of courage and fortune magnifying other people's complacency, inadequacy and lacklustre life to cause conflict.

Some possessors of this attitude have deep-seated insecurity and use the façade of command and control as a camouflage. The cases of school bullies have been borne out as insecurity playing out on smaller classmates. We had a lady who tried to dominate every interaction and control decisions even when she was not part of the committee. However, we later witnessed that she could not stand up to her own teenage daughter whom she taught and trained as a tyrant. The seed of control finally came home to roost and she did not like the eggs it laid for her. She learnt what Laura Hillenbrand said, that "you cannot dominate the indomitable spirit of man by aggression, fear or intimidation."

Reaction to people

They like their authoritative domineering selves. However, they don't accord others the respect, honour and appreciation they deserve. Consequently, they too are dishonoured and disrespected. As business executives, they are the godfathers not to be crossed. They reign through fear instead of respect. As friends, they are the dominant but silent partner of the relationship. Everything must be for their sole interest. As co-workers, they direct others to work but do nothing to help. As bosses, they are overbearing. Consequently, they alienate the independent souls who know who they are and are freed from tyrannical rules. They also delay progress and productivity by hindering valuable contributions from others. They fail to appreciate the contribution others make or value them so many would-be helpers leave. From our studies, 2% of participants dislike overbearing, domineering people.

With all power and authority concentrated at the top, when the head cannot function, for whatever reason, everything grinds to a halt. Thus, they don't succeed in life because they don't allow successors to develop, grow, flourish or be trained in their presence. Therefore, many leave a legacy of infamy and shambles.

Their insecurity and fear of loosing control make them so pedantic, rigid and legalistic in nature that no one can reason with them. They subject all around to rigid routines to dominate them. But opportunities don't come from routines, they come during crisis and uncertainties. Hence, many who work with them miss their chances to grow and succeed. Blinded by power, they fail to see the error of their ways until too late.

*"He who exercises government by means of his virtue may
be compared to the north polar star,
which keeps its place and all the stars turn towards it."*
Confucius

*"If you once forfeit the confidence of your fellow citizens,
you can never regain their respect or esteem."*
Abraham Lincoln

*"We awaken in others the same attitude of mind we hold
toward them."*
Elbert Hubbard

*"Seek out that particular mental attribute which makes you
feel most deeply and vitally alive,
along with which comes the inner voice that says,
'This is the real me,'
and when you have found that attitude, follow it."*
James Truslow Adams

Chapter 12
The Caring attitude [Hen]

He knows the universe and himself he does not know
Jean de La Fontaine

These are the present day Marthas. They are energetic and bubble with enthusiasm. Their attitude in life is a selfless, servant service fixing everyone. They get involved with delinquents, aggressive and abusive people because they think they can just fix and change them by loving them. They spend sleepless nights worrying about the extinction of the alligators in the reservations in America and the emission of toxic waste in the remote areas of the Andes. Yet, they take very little thought for their own welfare. Thus, undue worry and needless anxiety in service are their hallmarks.

Purposeful living

Possessors of this attitude are great worriers. Their purpose in life is to oversee the universe and ensure that everything and everyone functions as preordained and created. They live life to the full because they have a lot to oversee and attend to. They can demonstrate and lobby anyone for their pet projects. Some are carers.

Reaction to challenges, risk and change

They face challenges squarely and sometimes take unnecessary steps to save the whales and the environment at great personal risks. They embrace change as opportunity to get something done. Some are fearless and determined with good reason. They usually struggle until they achieve their goals. For them Heraclitus' dictum "It is in changing that things find purpose" is a mantra.

Personal attributes

They are self-reliant and self-motivated, but lack self-confidence in personal matters. Like Biblical Martha, they are easily distracted by serving the needs of others. They are eternal mothers, or hens that regard others as children to be nurtured like chicks. However, some fail to realise that they can suffocate those who want space to live and breathe. They are mostly in the caring professions as nurses, doctors, social workers and volunteers in charitable organisations.

Many are simple, shy and ordinary kind-hearted people when they can be more. Some remain unmarried and unattached by default. They lack the courage and confidence to make decisions that will affect them, but can easily give good advice and suggestions to improve other people's lives. Consequently, they can be taken advantage of by family members. For example, they are the ones to care for aging parents and sick relatives. Since they have no families of their own, relatives dump their wards and responsibilities on them as benevolent aunties!

In their selfless, submissive attitude some fail to tend their vineyards because they are too busy working on others. Thus, they seem to neglect their health, outlook, own interests and homes. They are very good friends, confidants and relatives due to their caring and selfless nature. They are the perfect second fiddlers because they detest the limelight. They are happy to think, plan and execute projects faultlessly from behind the scenes and allow bosses to take credit for their effort. Like biblical Barnabas, Stephanas, Fortunatus and Achaicus (1 Corinthians 16:17-18), they are great encouragers. Thus, while some are busy saving the planet, others are serving and caring. They work well and make very good friends with the blasé.

Reaction to people

As co-workers, they do their share and more. As bosses, they will not delegate what they are not prepared to do themselves. As leaders, they don't know how to delegate. Consequently, they overwork to exhaustion and early burn out. They are God-sent to the lazy, pitiful and fearful in attitude; they care for them and smother them with affection.

Relationships should be mutually beneficial, but these "Marthas" are happy to oblige others to their own detriment. They are very good listeners and givers. They can use their last resource to help another soul. They are the unsung heroes of any age. They will go where no one is prepared to go and do menial jobs others abrogate. They are willing to spend and be spent on behalf of others or humanity.

Some have abandoned the world and all its competition and struggle to serve in convents and monasteries. They are the likes of Brother Lawrence, the French monk who discovered an overwhelming presence of God in his kitchen as a cook and in his shed as a cobbler to other monks. He made himself nothing so that God can be ALL in everything. They are the most potent intercessors. They have the willingness, time, energy, passion and a merciful heart to pray for others and see them healed or victorious without ever letting anyone know their contribution. Thus, they are the best prayer partners anyone could wish for. They know how to fight on behalf of others and stand by them until victory comes. May the Almighty, who sees in secret, reward these secret warriors and bless them in all they do for others - Amen.

Chapter 13
The Critical attitude [Carrion Crow]

Any fool can criticise and most fools do
Dale Carnegie

This is the attitude of the rebellious. It is the deceptive, divisive, supplanting spirit of Biblical Absalom. Its chief aim is to divide and rule. It is a selfish, self-seeking attitude of the people-pleaser, who deludes himself that he is as good as anyone or better. The hallmark of this attitude is a deceptive hunger for power rooted in criticism. They deceitfully slander to kill with word and tongue as with the sword. Like Doeg the Edomite did to King David and ended up slaying eighty five priests of Nob to taint David's character and ingratiate himself with King Saul (1 Samuel 22:6-23). In the end, his sins found him out and he paid dearly for it.

Purposeful living

Possessors of this attitude crave personal aggrandisement at others' detriment. Their life purpose is to dispossess others and seize what they laboured for. It may be the throne, as in the case of Absalom, or fame and fortune in others. They scheme and plot to discredit and shame others through criticism in order to replace them. They are ambitious, motivated by greed, on a mission to prove that they can do better.

Reaction to challenges, risk and change

They enjoy the challenge of dispossessing others and supplanting them. The thrill of the chase seems to gratify them. They embrace change to feather their nests at a cost to others. They are aggressive in competition and can mount a rebellion to achieve their dissention. By their action, they effect change, but of what kind?

Carrion crow critically analyses even a dead fly

Personal attribute

Possessors of this attitude are overconfident in their duplicity. They can be easily offended and seek revenge. To prove their ability to do better, they criticise those in authority to discredit them before subordinates and so ingratiate themselves with the masses who they lead astray. They misrepresent information so others arrive at the wrong conclusions. They manage to sow seed of discord and dissatisfaction among church members, families, subordinates and friends. Thus, they gather disaffected, disgruntled and discontent followers to their cause and offer "better solutions" than the leaders.

In their pursuit of personal recognition and self-aggrandisement, they often challenge authority and seek to destabilise unity. Murmuring and complaints are rife. For example, Absalom deceived his father and captivated two hundred elders of the Sanhedrin to mount an insurrection against the king. Similarly, others deceive family or church members and friends to gang up against parents, leaders and others. In the end, they are all destroyed like Absalom, by their pride and deceitful attitude.

In their competitiveness they can block others' progress and seek to establish their own. When their goals go awry, they get angry and scheme to out stage others through slander, deceit and tale-bearing. Through fault-finding, they tarnish others' image and devalue their work to shame them. Thus, they capture sympathisers to their cause and scheme to reject the leader in their favour.

Some may seek personal recognition and affiliation with influential bosses to legitimise their case. For example, Korah and his cohorts who rose up against Moses and Aaron's authority is a case in point. He thought they were all equal and capable of leading the nation. God thought otherwise and destroyed him with the elders who joined his rebellion (Numbers 16). Thus, the saying that "every carrion crow, will crow on its own dunghill" was confirmed.

Possessors of this critical attitude lack a worthy character. They are disloyal to elected authority, disrespectful and dishonourable. Because they have questionable character, they cannot submit to authority. When their ideas and pet projects are rejected, they feel a personal affront. Jealousy spurs them on to criticise or viciously slander and become disagreeable. Carter Godwin Woodson noted that "men of lesser magnetism are easily provoked to jealousy when others make in roads in areas they think they are more competent." Thus their lacklustre character compounds failure to reveal their aggression. As King David observed, "Man is a dangerous foe. He feigns outward friendship while in his heart he is a bitter implacable foe" (see Psalm 55:10).

They do not cooperate with existing programmes because cooperation, writes Carter Godwin Woodson, "implies equality of participation in the task at hand." In their delusion and arrogance, they think they can do better and spend their time criticising and condemning, rather than cooperating with others' ideas and programmes.

Reaction to people

Pride and arrogance do not allow possessors of this attitude to cooperate with others. Therefore, they avoid people or are indifferent, except to enlist them in their causes. They desire to lead others even when they lack the vision and qualities needed to do so. Unfortunately for those led astray, the splinter group eventually succumbs to the path of least resistance and evolves only to experience the full force of deception and hidden flaws of their critical leader. In our experience, families and communities have been disrupted and divided by criticism and fault-finding in elected leaders. The new groups soon found out that their new leaders deceived them and were worse than those they left. The grass is not always greener on the other side of the fence.

It is always easier to criticise, complain and discourage, but much better to appreciate, complement and celebrate others, no matter how meagre the contribution and accomplishment. But those with this attitude in relationships choose to unload their wrong attitude on unfortunate mates and associates. As drama kings or queens, they are there to be served and validated and offer no affection, gratitude, respect, appreciation or acknowledgement in return. Unfortunately, those they terrorise are basically fearful and lack the initiative and self-assertion to counter their misery and pain. Consequently, the critical can get away with wrong attitude, but for a season, hurting the vulnerable and weak.

The previous ten attitude types were elicited from our varied experiences and confirmed by our survey. The names of the people are withheld because many are still alive. Read through these unfortunate attitudes again and again and really analyse your own attitude. If you need to make changes for a more pleasing attitude and personality, then please do so.

Many may disregard or trifle with them and think they belong to others. We have found that many people exhibit aspects of very negative attitude, yet are either unaware or in denial about them. Consequently, their relationships suffer and they often wonder why. Do you not see that change is needed when we attract what we really are instead of the happiness, joy, peace, harmonious relationships we desire? Do you not see that a small change in conduct can lead to success of your quest, instead of trial and error? Do you not see that we can only change our own attitude and in time we will attract people of similar attitude? We all have choices; choose wisely.

The next chapter deals with the changing of negative attitudes to desired ones through reflection, analysis, acceptance and forgiveness. It has helped many to change for the better and can help you too.

Chapter 14
Choosing an appropriate attitude

It will pay anyone to stand on the sidelines of life and watch himself go by so he may see himself as others see him

Napoleon Hill

Introduction

When you know yourself as you are known, you are deemed wise and mature. Then like King Lear in Shakespeare, you will not ask "Who can tell me who I am?" You will know. The essence of reading about the ten attitude types is to examine your attitude and decide if it is serving you well. If you are fortunate to have developed a worthy character (attitude), I rejoice with you. If, however, you need to adjust or change your inappropriate attitude for a more appropriate one, then this 21 days' exercise is for you. A Chinese philosopher, Confucius, noted that "Only the most intelligent and the most stupid do not change." For us mortals, change is constant. For in changing, we find meaning and purpose to things. "Those who are through with change are simply through," writes Heraclitus. Therefore, change is important to liberate us from the past.

Why 21 days? It takes 21 days to change a habit and replace it with another one. Human beings are creatures of habit. We love the familiar, regular and routine. I used it to change my impatient attitude and it worked well for me. Others have used it to change their attitude, find purpose in life, restore broken relationships and liberate their minds from strongholds like fear. Try it and you may be glad you did.

Reflection and self-analysis

A life unexamined is not worth living

Plato's dictum

Spend seven days reflecting and analysing your attitude. Has your attitude served you well? Are you happy with all that you are? Do you love, cherish, value, honour, and esteem all that you are? Perhaps like Augustine, you can say "I myself do not grasp all that I am." This is a chance to reflect and know. Do you accept all your experience, the good, not so good and ugly? With acceptance comes freedom.

You need to identify your dominant attitude, what is its source? How did you acquire it? Where did things go wrong for you? What is your desire now? To master your enemy, you must know his name, habits and place of abode. Then you can plan a strategy to engage and overcome him. Similarly, you need to identify areas of your attitude that need adjustment or change. Decide on a desired alternative and be willing to adjust and change for the better. All the past experiences that happened to you are necessary to make you all that you are today.

Examine them and learn valuable lessons from them. Those who criticised and judged you, analyse what they said. Is it true, praiseworthy, honourable and of good report? Accept them. If what they said was false and unhelpful, disregard and clear them from your memory by replacing them with who you know you are. Until you deal with and break from the past, you cannot plan for the future or enjoy the present and you will be bound to repeat past mistakes.

De-clutter your mind and emotions

If you forgive others when they sin against you,
your heavenly Father will also forgive you.
But if you do not forgive others their sin,
your Father will not forgive your sins

Mathew 6:14-15

Spend the next seven days pondering and de-cluttering your mind and emotions. Forgiveness is the purpose of de-cluttering the mind. "As you think, so are you and as you continue to think, so you will remain," says James Allen. To make room for new attitude, you need to jettison the old one with all its baggage of anger, hatred, fears, bitterness, resentment, envy, jealousy, shame, worry, anxiety, discontentment, doubt, mistrust, indifference apathy and despair. You cannot put new wine into old wine bottles, or they will burst.

"Nature has endowed mankind with absolute control over his thoughts," says Napoleon Hill. It is the only area we control. So you are in charge of all your thoughts. You hold the key to let in weed of unhealthy thoughts into your mind. You also have the power to plant desirable corn or wheat in the fertile ground of your mind. Perhaps you have inadvertently sown unhealthy weed of negative emotions. We all did that because we knew no better. But now we know better, we must weed out the negative so that the positive we desire can grow and flourish.

We owe everyone a debt of love that we can never pay. It is irrelevant whether they accept our kindness and love, reciprocate them or not. Just you do your duty to love all and do no harm to your neighbour and you have fulfilled the entire law of the universe! It is so simple; many employed the use of sages to misunderstand and misinterpret nature. If our debt is to love all others, do you not see that there is no room for hatred, anger, bitterness, resentment and acrimony? True love (not human emotional love) is not fretful, conceited or touchy. It keeps no record of wrongs and pays no attention to any wrong it suffers. Consequently, love is kind, gentle, patient and enduring. It entertains no envy or jealousy, is not resentful, boastful or haughty. It believes the best of everyone without judging them; bears up under all circumstances and endures all insults without weakening. Thus, it never fades and never fails, for it is neither selfish nor self-seeking (1 Corinthians 13:1-8 AMP). Such love demands unending forgiveness. The recommended rate is (70X7) or X490 per day!

But unforgiveness mires you in a defeated attitude of bitter hatred. It is a way to control others and make them pay. Forgiveness benefits you more than those you forgive. It releases you from being the jailer of those who wronged you. It breaks the connection between you and them. It liberates you from the ugly pain of the past. It relieves you of the baggage and bondage of past mistakes and bitter resentment. It enables you to regain freedom to live and love again. You will unburden yourself. The heavy weight of dead issues of the past will drop like lead from your shoulders. You have the key. You can decide by your will to forgive everyone who wronged you NOW. Do it now and get it over with. Good. Feel free. Feel liberated. Be revitalised.

Rejoice. It is a new day. The cold ash of the past is dumped. Shout with the voice of triumph. Now decide never to entertain bitter or angry thoughts ever again against anyone. It does not matter what they do. You are not their judge. We cannot change others. We are only responsible for ourselves.

"The most beautiful thing you can do is to forgive a wrong done by others and yourself," says a Jewish Rabbi. It is the exercise of mercy. William Blake noted that "mercy has a human heart," like yours. Well done.

Let the joy of forgiveness and the peace that is its fruit flood and wash over your heart and mind. You can grieve and mourn if need be. You have lived with negative emotions for so long. Losing them is a real loss. Even the brave shed tears. You need rest from your painful past and freedom from bondage and misery.

Fill up with appropriate attitude

We must first be our own before we can be another's
Ralph Waldo Emerson

Spend the last seven days filling up with a more appropriate attitude for your need. You are now yourself, having unburdened the dead bodies you have carried about. You need to open yourself up to love and be loved. This is the way of the universe. Many people cannot love others because they have never been loved. There is no reference point. You cannot give what you have not experienced or have. But God so loved the world that He gave His only son to us. It is the greatest act of love to those that don't care and even hate Him. He has always loved and will always love people created in His image and likeness. But many do not receive His unconditional, free, constant and unending love. So they don't like who they are. They loathe or dislike themselves. They wish they were someone else! We found 27% of them in our survey. What a pity.

They are indifferent to other people so they avoid them. George Bernard Shaw calls indifference, "The worst sin and the essence of inhumanity." People undervalue themselves. They dishonour and disrespect themselves. They project an attitude of self-loathing and wonder why the public treats them as such. So start loving yourself. The public will treat you as they find you.

Value, esteem, honour, respect and accept all that you are. Be happy and satisfied in your own skin. You must be whole before you can venture to relate meaningfully with others. All that you are and have experienced are needed to fulfil your life purpose. Learn to accept and love all that you are. They make you a unique, special one of a kind creature, unrepeatable and distinguished. Be proud of all that.

In life, those who cannot receive and accept the love of God (vertical acceptance) cannot love themselves and therefore cannot love others (horizontal acceptance). The heart of man was created by God for Himself. He alone can fill that inner void. Nothing in the whole universe can replace that hunger for divine love, because it is the ultimate nature of your spirit being. So first fill up with divine love to help you to love yourself. Proud pursuit of empty glory and accomplishments will never satisfy you. It has never satisfied anyone.

When you accept, value, love and honour yourself, the ephemeral love of man will pale in significance. The love of your neighbour is an overflow of your feeling of worth, value and esteem. As Augustine so poignantly put it:

"Late have I loved you O' beauty, so ancient and so new
Late have I loved you

You were within me and I was outside
and there I sought you"

William Wordsworth confirmed it when he wrote, "Strive not to banish pain and doubt, in pleasure's noisy din. The peace thou seek from without is only found within." Many people seek outside themselves and from other humans the love and peace only God can give for "our hearts are restless until they rest in Him."

Having filled up with divine love, peace of mind is its fruit to you. Like Augustine, you can cry out saying:

"You called and cried out to me and broke my deafness
You shone forth upon me and shattered my blindness
I tasted and I hunger and thirst
You touched me and I burned for your peace"

Thus without God's love and pursuit of life purpose, we are barren (worthless). But with His love and ensuing peace, we become fruitful in productive enjoyment (worthy).

Focus attention on the implications of your desired attitude on achieving your goals. Set yourself small meaningful but achievable goals to change. Persevere until goal is attained. Be determined to reach your goal and no hindrance will stand in your way. All that is worthy for you, you must work out for yourself. Persistence is the road to possessing.

Visualise the ultimate condition you hope to achieve and keep focusing on it as you progress to your ultimate desired attitude.

Make the exchanges

- Let the purposeless find a purpose. It's the reason and meaning for living
- For the hated and rejected, let there be acceptance of and delight in self
- For the apathetic and indifferent, let there be interest and care for others
- For worried minds, be calm
- For the anxious, let serenity reign
- For the prideful, don't be ashamed but be confident
- Let the frustrated find fulfilment
- The provoked, be appeased
- Let the sorrowful be joyful, life is sweet
- Let the doubting learn to trust more
- Where disagreement and aggression was, let peace flourish
- Let the despairing be hopeful, for the best is yet to come
- The angry and bitter, continue to forgive. You owe it to yourself
- The critic, judge and condemn no more, rather accept and celebrate others
- Let the fearful fear no more. Learn to believe and trust yourself.

- Let the indecisive make a decision. Even a wrong decision is better than none.
- Procrastinators wake up and dither no more. Only actions get results
- Domineering control freaks let go. Concentrate on yourself
- Deceitful who supplant, develop own gifts and talents and be happy with yours
- Tale-bearers, find more useful work for your valuable time and tongue
- Jealous and envious, covet no more. You can be more with a little effort
- Poverty-stricken and needy, look to your Maker; He is gracious and kind
- Distracted Martha, care more for yourself
- Self-made victims, arise and pity-party no more. You are more than your past

As you make the exchanges, continue to think according to the new attitude you want to inculcate. Talk in terms of it and allow yourself to feel like you have attained it. Act in the manner expected of those with that attitude. Then walk the talk. The moment you believed you could change, the change was already effected. The mind is supreme. As Art Williams said, "If you can believe it, you can do it." And "Whatever you are willing to fight for, nature will hand to you" says Andrew Carnegie.